THE BLUNT TRUTH

IF I TELL YOU WHERE I WANT TO SEE MYSELF
IN FIVE YEARS, IT MIGHT NEVER HAPPEN.

ANUBBHHAV RAJ

To everyone who has ever felt lost, misunderstood, or caught
between who they are and who they think they should be.

This book is for you—the ones who question everything, who stumble
and fall, and who somehow find the courage to get back up. You are
not alone.

And to my friends, whose love and support helped me find my way
through the darkest moments. Your belief in me, even when I didn't
believe in myself, has been my greatest gift.

Thank you for walking with me on this journey.

Contents

Contents

Acknowledgements

A huge thanks to my friends, Om Mishra, Kaustubh Vatsa, and Samarth Goyal—without you, this book would've been a collection of random thoughts.

I would also like to thank QuillBot, Grammarly, and MS Word for tirelessly correcting my poor grammar..

Disclaimer

This is a work of fiction. While inspired by real events and individuals, all characters in this book are fictitious, and any resemblance to actual people, living or dead, is purely coincidental. Names, characteristics, places, and incidents either are products of the author's imagination or are used fictitiously. The events, locations, and personal histories depicted herein have been modified, transformed, and reimagined through the lens of creative storytelling. Certain real-world elements have been altered, compressed, or expanded to serve the narrative purpose of this work. The portrayals of alcohol consumption, tobacco and other drugs within this book are part of the narrative context and should not be interpreted as an endorsement of such behaviors. Readers are reminded that the depiction of these substances is purely within the realm of fictional storytelling.

CHAPTER ONE

THE DREAM BEGINS

I can still feel the weight of that moment—the trolley in one hand, a bag on my shoulder, and a strange mix of exhaustion and excitement swirling inside me. It was early morning, around 6 AM, when I reached the main gate of IIT Delhi. After a 22-hour journey, my body was drained, but my mind? My mind was alive with thoughts, memories, and the overwhelming realization: *I made it.*

For three years, my life had been about one thing—cracking the IIT-JEE. I had locked myself away, completely isolated, studying from dawn till midnight. No school, no social life, just me, my books, and a ₹9,000 phone that I bought with the scholarship money I had earned for topping high school. It wasn't just a grind; it was survival. Every day was a reminder of what was at stake. And now, standing in front of the gates of IIT Delhi, it felt like all those sacrifices had led me here.

The guard handed me some documents to fill out and asked which hostel I was assigned to. "Kumaon," I replied. A small smile crept onto my face as the name sank in. Kumaon wasn't just any hostel; it was the home of legends. Chetan Bhagat, Ashneer Grover, SV Divakar—people who had walked these halls, lived in these rooms, and carved their names into history. I wondered if one day, someone might say the same about me.

Stepping into the campus was surreal. After being confined to a single room for years, the vastness of IIT Delhi felt overwhelming. The roads stretched endlessly before me, lined with trees that seemed to whisper stories of the students who had walked them before. I kept walking, pulling my trolley along the path, and then I saw it—the iconic main building. I had stared at its image on my screen countless times, dreaming of this moment. But seeing it in person was different. It wasn't just a building; it was a symbol of everything I had worked for.

When I finally reached Kumaon Hostel, I was greeted with a mix of warmth and formality. The seniors introduced me to the hostel's culture, its quirks, and its history. They shared stories of the alumni, the traditions, and what it meant to be part of Kumaon. There was no ragging, only friendly guidance, but despite their kindness, I felt out of place.

This wasn't because of them. It was because of me.

I wasn't always like this. Back in my school days, I was outgoing and full of confidence. I loved talking to people, making them laugh, and being part of the group. But those years of homeschooling and isolation during JEE preparation had changed me. I had spent so much time alone, immersed in my studies, that now, standing in a room full of new faces, I didn't know how to start a conversation. I wanted to talk, to connect, but something inside me held back.

Life at IIT started slowly. The excitement of arriving soon gave way to the reality of academics. Cracking the JEE wasn't the finish line—it was just the beginning. Here, the competition didn't end. Classes were intense, assignments kept piling up, and the expectations were relentless. I realized I'd have to study even harder than I had during JEE prep. And honestly, I was tired. I had been running on empty for years, and now the exhaustion was catching up to me.

Two months passed in a blur. I kept to myself, trying to find my footing in this new world. I wasn't unhappy, but I wasn't exactly thriving either. Then, as the end of the year approached, something shifted. It was New Year's Eve—the first real celebration of my new life at IIT. I didn't know it yet, but this night would mark the start of something that would change my story forever.

A NIGHT TO REMEMBER

I was living on the ground floor of Kumaon Hostel, and it was December 31st—New Year's Eve. The day had been uneventful, but that night, as the hours crept closer to midnight, I started hearing commotion from upstairs. Footsteps, hurried voices, and the unmistakable buzz of something big happening filled the air. Curiosity got the better of me, and I decided to check it out.

I climbed to the first floor and saw people rushing around, carrying things—bottles, bags, and crates—toward the stairs. I tried to ask someone what was going on, but they were too busy to respond. Then I spotted Malik, one of my batchmates.

"What's happening?" I asked.

"We're throwing a party," he said casually. "On the terrace."

That was all the invitation I needed. I followed him upstairs, my excitement building with every step.

When I reached the terrace, I stopped in my tracks. The scene in front of me was unlike anything I had ever experienced in my 19 years of life. There were people everywhere, bottles of beer and hard liquor lined up on a table, bowls of chips scattered around, and a small fire where they were grilling chicken. The air smelled like smoke, alcohol, and something new—freedom.

I wandered into the crowd, awkward but curious. It didn't take long before I struck up a conversation with two guys—Shaan Bansal, AIR 92 in JEE Advanced, and his twin brother Shayan Bansal, AIR 69. They were drinking and laughing like they had nothing to worry about, and they seemed like genuinely good people.

"Want to try?" one of them asked, holding out a beer bottle.

I hesitated for a second, then said, "Yes." It was my first drink ever.

The moment I took a sip, I regretted it. The taste was horrible—bitter and fizzy in the worst way. But I pretended to be cool, acting like I could handle it. When no one was looking, I quietly left the bottle in a corner.

Determined to keep exploring, I decided to try something else. Someone handed me a glass of Smirnoff vodka. I took a sip, and it burned all the way down my throat. But then something happened. After a few more sips, I felt a sudden warmth in my body—a strange rush of excitement. I felt... confident. For the first time in forever, I had the courage to step onto the dance floor.

I started dancing—wildly, freely, without caring what anyone thought. It had been so long since I had danced, I didn't even know if I was doing it right. But none of that mattered. The energy on the terrace was electric, and I was part of it.

Suddenly, someone started counting down: "10, 9, 8..." Everyone joined in, including me. When we hit "1," the entire terrace erupted with shouts of "Happy New Year!" People hugged each other, cheering and laughing.

A guy I didn't recognize hugged me and said, "Happy New Year!" They called him PDS. He wasn't from Kumaon but another hostel. His energy was magnetic. Everyone seemed drawn to him, and he was enjoying himself, radiating confidence and ease. In the back of my mind, I thought, *This could be me.*

As I soaked in the atmosphere, I noticed someone sitting in the corner, weeping. A small crowd gathered around him, trying to console him. Apparently, he was crying over his ex. I stood back, watching the scene, and honestly, I couldn't take it seriously. To me, it seemed like he just wanted attention. I laughed to myself, thinking, *This guy isn't even crying properly.*

Meanwhile, I decided to try whiskey, thinking it might be better than vodka. It wasn't. Then I tried rum. Same result. But even though I didn't like any of the drinks, I felt oddly accomplished, like I was ticking items off some invisible checklist.

Time flew by, and before I knew it, some seniors arrived on the terrace. We had been too loud, and they were there to shut things down before the guards got involved. One of them, Aaryan Oganja, was a well-known figure in the IIT. He stepped in, calm and collected, and took charge of the situation.

"Alright, party's over," he said firmly but not unkindly. "Everyone, clean up and get back to your rooms before the guards show up."

I couldn't help but admire him. He had this balance of authority and coolness, the kind of senior you looked up to.

By then, I was a little tipsy—not drunk, just enough to feel lightheaded. But I noticed something funny: the people who were really drunk were getting all the attention. So, I decided to act the part. I stumbled a bit, slurred my words,

and let one of my peers help me back to my room.
    On the way, I confessed, "I didn't like alcohol at all."
    He laughed and said, "Then you should try weed."

• 7 •

CHAPTER THREE

A NEW MORNING, A NEW OBSESSION

I woke up late—around 2 PM—and felt like every bone in my body was cracking. My muscles ached from the way I'd danced the night before. Every movement reminded me of how crazy that night had been. I dragged myself out of bed and realized the mess would close soon. Panicking, I rushed out, still groggy, and made it just in time before they shut the doors.

Sitting there, I tried to eat, but I wasn't really hungry. The excitement of the night still buzzed in my mind, making it hard to focus on food. I somehow managed to finish two slices of bread before heading back to my room.

Lying on my bed, I couldn't stop thinking about the party. The music, the laughter, the energy—it all replayed in my head like a movie. I imagined different versions of what had happened, embellishing the details in my mind, like introverts often do. That's when a thought popped up: *Smirnoff.*

The vodka had left an impression on me. I didn't like the taste at first, but there was something about it—maybe the warmth it left behind or the fire it lit in my veins. I had to try it again.

Excited, I rushed to the first floor, where the cooler people of my year lived. People like Samarth. That day was the first time I formally spoke to him. He was friendly enough, but when I asked if he had any Smirnoff left, he just shrugged and said, "It's finished."

"Where'd you get it?" I asked.

"It's 300 bucks for a hipster red Smirnoff—180 ml," he replied casually.

I was stunned. "300? That's so cheap," I thought to myself. It felt like a golden opportunity slipping away. I returned to my room, my mind spinning with ways to get my hands on a bottle.

The Plan

Suddenly, I remembered a guy who lived next to me: Ekraj Agarwal. I didn't know him well, but in IIT, most conversations followed a script anyway—"What's your name? Where are you from? What branch are you in?" That was about the depth of it. I decided to drop by his room for a chat, hoping I could work my way toward the topic of alcohol.

"Hey, Ekraj," I started casually. "You were at the party last night, right?"

"Yeah, it was crazy," he said, laughing.

One thing led to another, and soon enough, alcohol came into the conversation.

"Let's drink something," he said.

I couldn't believe my luck. "Do you have anything?" I asked eagerly.

"No," he replied. "But we can buy some."

Excitement bubbled up inside me. "Let's go," I said without a second thought.

The First Trip to the Liquor Store

At that moment, I realized I didn't have any money. I called my cousin sister and asked her to send me ₹1,000 on Paytm. It was the first time in my life I'd asked anyone for money. I had always been careful, never needing much, but this felt different. As I hung up, a strange thought hit me: *Am I doing something wrong?*

But the excitement of buying alcohol drowned out the doubt. Ekraj and I left the hostel and walked to the nearest liquor shop in Munirka, about a kilometer away.

When we got there, the scene was chaotic. The shop was packed with people—men jostling for space, a few women browsing casually, and the shopkeeper barking orders to his staff. It was a completely new experience for me.

I hesitated as we approached the counter. The shopkeeper glanced at me, his eyes narrowing slightly.

"Sir, please leave the store," he said firmly.

Confused, I stepped back. That's when Ekraj explained: "You can't buy alcohol legally until you're 25."

The realization hit me like a slap. Not only was I trying alcohol for the first time, but I was also doing something illegal. Fear crept in. I started imagining the police showing up, interrogating me, arresting me—my mind raced with worst-case scenarios.

At 19 years old, I was already self-conscious about looking younger than my age. People often said I looked 16, and now that thought came back to haunt me. *No wonder the shopkeeper didn't believe me,* I thought bitterly.

Ekraj, on the other hand, had no trouble. With his beard and confident demeanor, he looked older—probably 22 or so. He managed to buy the alcohol while I waited nervously outside, scanning for any signs of the police.

When he walked out with the bottle in his hand, I felt a surge of happiness. It was as if he'd just won a prize for both of us.

Back at the Hostel

We returned to the hostel, stopping along the way to buy soft drinks and chips to go with the alcohol. Back in Ekraj's room, we settled in and started drinking.

The first sip of vodka burned as much as it had the night before, but this time, I was ready for it. The familiar warmth spread through my body, and soon I was singing and dancing, just like I had at the party.

Eventually, I left Ekraj's room, still humming and swaying. The lights in my room were off, but I didn't mind. My mind was buzzing with excitement and something else—a thought that seemed to come out of nowhere: *A girl.*

Was it love? Attraction? Or just a fleeting idea brought on by the alcohol? I couldn't tell, but the thought lingered as I lay on my bed, staring at the ceiling and replaying the night in my head.

CHAPTER FOUR

THE RISE OF THE NASHEDI

Time passed, and my drinking habits escalated. By now, I had started day drinking regularly. College classes became a distant memory—I rarely attended anymore. Instead, I found myself in my room, bottle in hand, sipping vodka that could get me tipsy with just 60–90ml. My tolerance was laughably low, which made it oddly cost-effective.

At first, it felt like a harmless escape. In January and early February, alcohol became a constant companion. I wasn't drinking excessively by most people's standards, but it was *a lot* for me. Word spread around Kumaon Hostel, and soon people knew me as the guy who day drinks. I became a small-time celebrity, with whispers of "nashedi" floating around the hostel halls.

The Realization at Home

After weeks of this routine, the semester ended, and I went home for a short 10-day break. The holiday gave me time to reflect, and the reality of my situation started sinking in. Sitting in my room at home, I couldn't help but compare the person I had become to the person I used to be. I remembered my school days, when I always scored above 90%, driven by ambition and discipline. Now, in my first semester at IIT, I had barely scraped by with a 5.6 CGPA.

I hadn't studied much—just crammed a day before the exams—and somehow managed to pass. It wasn't that I wasn't capable; I just didn't care enough. Alcohol wasn't giving me what I really wanted. I was running from my responsibilities, from the life I had expected in college. My vision of IIT, of academic excellence and personal growth, was a far cry from the reality I was living.

On the train ride back to campus, I made a decision. *Things will change. I will go back to college, attend classes, and actually work toward something productive.*

Back to Campus

When I returned to college, I made an effort to attend classes. But it didn't take long to realize that classroom learning wasn't for me. I had always studied on my own, and sitting in lectures felt alien. I quickly lost interest and, once again, stopped going to class.

Around this time, I reconnected with a friend from my first semester, Harish. We were in the same group back then, and he somehow knew about my drinking habits. It seemed my reputation as a "nashedi" had spread far and wide.

"Do you have alcohol?" he asked one day.

I didn't, but I offered a solution. "We can buy some," I said.

It felt like déjà vu—the same situation I had been in months ago when I first ventured to Munirka to buy alcohol. Harish wasn't from my hostel, but he came over, and we made the familiar trip to the liquor store. This time,

I felt less nervous. Harish had a beard and looked older, so he handled the purchase while I waited outside.

Back in my room, we started drinking. Harish, who had never really drunk much before, took five shots of vodka and was completely drunk. He started saying things like, "You're my best friend," and showering me with compliments. I couldn't help but wonder: *When did this happen? Since when am I his best friend?*

It didn't take long to realize what was going on. Harish, like others, saw me as someone "popular" because of my drinking habits. To him, I was the guy everyone knew as a fun, carefree drinker. But the truth was far from that.

The Truth Behind the Nashedi

The reality was that I hadn't drunk as much as people thought. Over two months of drinking, I had consumed barely a liter of vodka in total. My tolerance was just so low that after one or two shots, I'd feel tipsy and start wandering from room to room, talking to people. It became a pattern: I'd drink, get slightly drunk, and then roam the hostel, chatting nonsense. My behavior made me noticeable, and people quickly associated me with drinking.

On top of that, I'd developed a habit of calling people after drinking, saying random things and talking mostly about a girl. It was always the same girl, the one I couldn't get out of my mind after my first vodka-fueled night.

All of this added to my so-called fame, but deep down, I knew it wasn't true. I wasn't the heavy drinker everyone thought I was. It was my behavior—not the amount of alcohol I consumed—that earned me the nickname "nashedi."

That night, after Harish left my room, I lay on my bed, thinking about everything. The whispers, the calls, the exaggerated reputation—it all played on repeat in my mind. I felt a strange mix of amusement and frustration.

The Call

As I lay there, lost in thought, my phone rang. It was Harish. My heart skipped a beat, and I hesitated before answering.

"Bro," he said, slurring slightly. "You gave me alcohol for the first time, so tomorrow... I'll give you your first cigarette."

His words hit me like a jolt. My mind raced. I wasn't sure if I was excited, nervous, or just plain curious.

THE FIRST CIGARETTE

It was a quiet evening, and I was sitting in my room, lost in thought. Daydreaming had become a habit of mine. Like many introverts, I often created elaborate scenarios in my mind—imagining myself in places I'd never been, doing things I'd never done. I pictured myself confidently talking to people, performing on stage, dancing in front of a crowd, or even singing. These daydreams were vivid, but they weren't real. They were my escape, a private world where I could be the person I wasn't in reality.

Suddenly, my phone rang. It was Harish.

"Bro, let's try a cigarette," he said, his tone casual but persuasive.

I hesitated for a second before replying, "Okay."

As I rushed to his hostel, a strange thought crossed my mind. I had an odd sense of ethics about doing *nasha*. In my head, I believed I should only indulge in one type of vice at a time. If I started smoking cigarettes, I'd have to quit alcohol. It was the kind of logic only a 19-year-old with little social experience could come up with.

The Journey to Jia Sarai

When I reached Harish's hostel, he was waiting for me. "There's a shop in Jia Sarai," he said. "We'll go through the small gate near the campus to get there."

We walked together, stepping outside the IIT campus through a narrow gate. Jia Sarai was a bustling area just outside the hostel, filled with tiny shops and the constant hum of activity. Among them was a small cigarette shop, barely big enough to stand in.

Harish asked the shopkeeper for a "Choti Advance" cigarette. The shopkeeper handed him one, and Harish lit it up without hesitation. He took a puff and then passed it to me.

"Just take a puff," he said, smiling.

I held the cigarette awkwardly and brought it to my lips. I took a small drag and immediately blew the smoke out. Harish laughed. "Bro, you're just mouthing it!"

I stared at him, confused. "What's mouthing?"

He explained that I wasn't inhaling the smoke properly—it was just staying in my mouth. I finished the cigarette like that, blowing out every puff without letting it reach my lungs. Nothing happened.

By the end of it, I was unimpressed. "This is it?" I asked. "Why do people even do this? Just for the smoke?" Harish shrugged, clearly amused. We laughed it off and walked back to campus.

A Lesson from a Senior

When I reached the guard desk of my hostel, I saw one of my seniors. He was kind and approachable, always ready to chat. His name was also Harish—a coincidence that didn't escape me.

"How are you? Where are you coming from?" he asked casually.

I didn't hesitate. "I just came back from outside the campus. Tried smoking a cigarette," I said, almost proudly.

He raised an eyebrow. "You smoke?"

"Well, I tried. But honestly, nothing happened," I replied. "Why do people even smoke?"

He smiled knowingly. "You probably didn't do it right. Come with me—I'll show you how."

Intrigued, I followed him. We left the campus through Gate No. 6 and walked to a small spot nearby called Sassi. Sassi was a no-frills place—a small setup selling nothing but cigarettes. The air around it was thick with smoke, and a steady stream of customers came and went.

Harish asked the shopkeeper for a Choti Advance cigarette. He lit it up and turned to me. "Here's how you do it," he said.

"First, take the smoke into your mouth. Don't exhale yet. Then open your mouth slightly and inhale air through it, pulling the smoke into your lungs. Don't exhale until you feel it."

I nodded, determined to get it right this time. He handed me the cigarette, and I followed his instructions carefully.

The first time, I felt nothing. The second time, it started to hit me. And on the third puff, everything changed.

The Feeling

A wave of sensation washed over me—warm, heady, and strange. My chest felt light, my head slightly dizzy, and my thoughts sharper. It was a completely different feeling from alcohol. It wasn't warmth or excitement; it was calm, focus, and a peculiar sense of control.

For a moment, I felt... better. I couldn't explain it, but it was as if a switch had flipped in my mind. I looked at Harish, who grinned knowingly.

"Now you get it," he said.

I nodded silently, taking another drag and letting the feeling settle in. For better or worse, this was the first time I truly understood why people smoked.

THE FIRST JOINT

Smoking had become my new routine. After leaving alcohol behind entirely, cigarettes took their place in my life. Every day, I found myself walking to Sassi, just three minutes away from the hostel. At first, one cigarette was enough to give me that euphoric "hit," a sense of focus and clarity that seemed to heighten everything. But as time passed, I noticed I was chasing that hit more and more, lighting up another cigarette as soon as the feeling faded.

Smoking became tied to everything I did. If I needed to study, I smoked. If I wanted to think clearly, I smoked. If I was bored, I smoked. It became less about the pleasure and more about the ritual, the escape it offered.

Finding a Hangout Spot

Around this time, I started spending more time in the cooler wing of the first floor—specifically, Room EB37. It belonged to Ayshu and his roommate, Samarth, but it had somehow turned into a communal hangout spot. Shaan, Shayan, Anmol Tiwari, Jitu Bansal, Shantanu, Peter, devansh and others all gathered there regularly. It was the kind of room where people came and went constantly, a place where conversations flowed as freely as the smoke.

At first, I didn't say much when I was there. I'd sit back, observing the banter and listening to their jokes, occasionally joining in with a laugh or a nod. But I kept going back. For one, cigarettes were always available there, and I enjoyed the company.

One day, when I was in EB37, I noticed a small remote-like device being passed around. Everyone was taking puffs from it. Curious, I asked, "What's that?"

"It's a vape," someone replied.

I tried it, taking a puff. It tasted different from cigarettes—not bad, just... different. I didn't like it much, but I kept puffing anyway, intrigued by the novelty of it. It was something new, and in a way, it felt like I was expanding my horizons, even if it was just in small ways.

A Routine Forms

My days started falling into a predictable pattern. I'd wake up around 11 AM and spend an hour scrolling through Instagram. Then I'd head to the mess for lunch at noon. After two hours of idle time, I'd go to the lab from 2 PM to 5 PM. Once the lab ended, I'd head straight to EB37, where I'd spend the rest of the evening and night—sometimes until 1 or 2 AM.

The hours in EB37 were filled with cigarettes, vapes, and endless conversations. I didn't talk much, but I listened intently, observing everyone around me. Their jokes, their arguments, their random musings—it all fascinated me.

One day, the topic of "weed" came up.

"Everyone should try weed at least once," someone said, sparking a lively discussion.

Most people in the room agreed, and I nodded along quietly. I didn't say much, but the idea planted itself in my mind. I wondered what it would feel like. Would it be like alcohol? Cigarettes? Something completely different?

House Day: The Real Party

Then came House Day, one of the biggest events in the hostel. It was a celebration where third-year students threw a party for the fourth-years, recognizing them with awards based on their achievements and contributions during their time in the hostel.

The official event started at 10 PM, but the real party began afterward. This was my first House Day party, and I didn't know what to expect. As I wandered through the hostel corridors, I noticed two rooms that had become the epicenters of the chaos.

One room was packed with alcohol. People were lining up to fill their glasses, stumbling out moments later with beers, whiskeys, and vodkas in hand. On the other side of the corridor was another room, where weed was being smoked. I didn't dare peek inside—there were too many seniors, and the sheer number of people coming and going was intimidating.

Instead, I left the corridor and went back to EB37.

The First Joint

When I entered, Samarth was lying on the bed, looking a little drunk. I sat next to him, and we started talking. Samarth had always been kind to me. He somehow understood my weaknesses without me ever having to explain them. He knew I wasn't great at starting conversations or making jokes, and he always made an effort to include me, to make me feel comfortable.

"You're not as quiet as you think," he said once, smiling. "You just don't realize it."

It was a reassuring thought, but in my head, I doubted it. I wondered if he was just being polite.

While we were talking, Ayshu—walked in. He was holding something small in his hand, and smoke was curling out of it. At first, I thought it was a half-burnt cigarette, but when I looked closer, I realized it was something else entirely.

"What's that?" I asked.

"This," he said with a grin, "is a joint."

My heart skipped a beat. This was the first time I had ever seen a joint up close. The way he held it, the casualness with which he took a puff, made it seem so normal. Yet, to me, it felt like a glimpse into an entirely new world.

CHAPTER SEVEN

THE FIRST HIGH

The joint passed from Ayshu to Samarth, who took three steady puffs before handing it back. Then, unexpectedly, Ayshu turned to me, holding the joint out with a knowing smile.

"Here, try it," he said.

I hesitated for a second, then took it. This wasn't a cigarette. The smoke was thicker, denser, and carried an earthy, unfamiliar taste. I drew four or five long drags, exhaling smoothly. It didn't hit me immediately—maybe because I was already used to cigarettes—but something about it felt different, heavier.

After Ayshu left, it was just me and Samarth in the room. For the first 15 minutes, everything felt normal. We were chatting casually when, out of nowhere, something shifted.

The Shift

I don't know what triggered it, but suddenly, I couldn't stop talking about a girl I'd seen on my first day of college. Let's call her Syra.

I had never been in love, never experienced the kind of romance they show in movies. But when I saw her that day in the lab, something stirred inside me. I didn't know her, had never spoken to her, but the image of her had lingered ever since.

"She was standing there," I told Samarth, my words spilling out faster than I could control. "In the lab, wearing a yellow sweater... I don't know, bro, it was just something about her. Do you think that's what love feels like?"

Samarth, to my surprise, opened up too. "You know, there was this girl," he said. "Laiba. Back in school. She's in Singapore now."

"What did you say to her?" I asked.

"I didn't say anything," he replied, staring at the ceiling.

Then it hit both of us at the same time.

"What did you say, bro?" he asked again.

"Nothing," I replied.

"No, seriously. What did you just say?"

"I said nothing!"

We looked at each other, wide-eyed. That's when we realized: *We're completely fucked up.*

The Hunger Hits

The high began to pull us into a different dimension. It wasn't like anything I'd ever felt before. My mind was floating, my thoughts scattered. There was no happiness or sadness, just... something else. A state of being that felt disconnected from reality yet strangely peaceful.

"Bro," Samarth said suddenly, "I'm hungry."

"Me too, bro," I replied.

Samarth decided to order pizza. What should have been a simple task turned into an epic adventure. We struggled to even find the food delivery app on his phone, spending five minutes just scrolling through random icons. Every time we thought we'd figured it out, something distracted us—a notification, a random thought, or just sheer confusion.

Finally, we managed to place the order, but by then we were too lost in our own minds to care. We lay on the bed, staring at the ceiling, feeling weightless and thoughtless. Time seemed to stretch infinitely, and for half an hour, we completely forgot we had even ordered anything.

The Call

Suddenly, Samarth's phone buzzed.

"Hello?" he answered.

"Sir, this is the delivery boy. I've arrived with your pizza," the voice on the other end said.

The phone was on speaker, and as the words sank in, we turned to each other and burst into uncontrollable laughter. We laughed so hard it felt like our lungs would give out. Somehow, we dragged ourselves to the guard desk at the hostel entrance, where the delivery boy was waiting.

The Pizza Debacle

The guard watched us curiously as we grabbed the pizza and sat down on the sofa at the entrance. Samarth opened the box, and the aroma of hot, cheesy pizza hit us like a wave.

I picked up a slice, took a bite, chewed it, and then froze. Something was wrong.

"Bro," I said, staring at Samarth, "I forgot how to swallow."

Samarth burst out laughing. "Bro, I forgot how to chew!"

The absurdity of it all sent us spiraling into another fit of laughter. The guard at the desk kept glancing at us, clearly trying to figure out what was going on.

"Bro," I whispered, "the guard is looking at us."

"Then stop looking at him," Samarth replied, deadpan. "If you don't look at him, he won't look at you."

It was the kind of logic that only made sense in that moment. I nodded seriously, determined to focus on the pizza. Eventually, we managed to eat it, bite by bite, swallowing carefully as if we were relearning how to eat for the first time.

Back to EB37

After finishing the pizza, we returned to EB37, our minds still swimming in the haze of the high. Samarth lay down on the bed, and I sat next to him, staring at the ceiling again. The night had been insane—unlike anything I'd ever experienced.

For the first time in my life, I felt like I had stepped into a completely different world, a world where time slowed down, where thoughts became dreams, and where the simplest things—like eating pizza—felt like an adventure.

That night, as I drifted off to sleep in EB37, I knew one thing for sure: this was just the beginning.

CHAPTER EIGHT

A MORNING OF REFLECTIONS

When I woke up that morning, my head felt heavy, my body too tired to move. I stumbled back to my room and collapsed onto my bed, trying to piece together the haze of memories from the previous night. Everything felt smoggy, as though the events were hidden behind a fogged glass. Still, one moment stood out—the conversation I had with Samarth.

For the first time in my life, I had shared my feelings about the girl I had seen on my first day of college. Her image had stayed with me—her yellow sweater, her quiet presence in the lab. And last night, under the influence of weed, I had let it all out. I told Samarth how I felt, the way she made me think about emotions I'd never allowed myself to feel.

Was it the weed that had pushed me to open up? Or was it just years of bottled-up emotions finally spilling over? I didn't know, but it was a strange relief—something I hadn't realized I needed. In my silent life, where emotions like love, sadness, or anger rarely surfaced, that release felt monumental.

I drifted back to sleep, lost in thoughts of her, the night, and the peculiar confidence weed had given me. When I woke again, it was already 8 PM. My stomach growled, and I headed to the mess for dinner, still feeling like I was floating in an unfamiliar mental space.

Back to EB37

After eating, I made my way to EB37, the unofficial hangout spot. As usual, Ayshu was glued to his laptop, typing furiously, while Samarth was lying on the bed, his MacBook resting on his chest in his signature way. The scene felt oddly comforting, familiar, even though I hadn't been part of it for long. At that time, I didn't know that one day, I'd be lying in the same way, with a laptop on my chest, engrossed in my own world.

"Bro, do you have a cigarette?" I asked Samarth.

Without looking up, he pointed toward a small rack near the corner of the room. I walked over, grabbed a cigarette from the pack, lit it, and took a long drag. The smoke swirled around me as I leaned against the wall, watching the two of them.

"Last night was crazy," I said, breaking the silence.

Samarth chuckled, his eyes still fixed on the screen. "Yeah, that was something different."

A Sudden Visitor

Just as the room was settling into its usual rhythm, the door burst open. It was Peter, looking unusually animated.

"Bro, my brother's here," he announced, grinning. "He's in my room. He's come from IIT Kharagpur."

There was no real reason for us to go, but for some reason, we all wanted to meet him. Maybe it was curiosity, maybe boredom. Either way, we left EB37 and made our way to Peter's room. When we arrived, his brother greeted us warmly, his demeanor confident yet easygoing.

We started with the usual small talk—questions about where we were from, how we were finding college life, and so on. But as the conversation flowed, it became clear that Peter's brother was someone who liked to get to the point.

"Do you guys do weed?" he asked suddenly, his tone casual.

I glanced at Samarth, and he looked at me. A small, knowing smile spread across our faces before we both replied, "Yes."

The next words were music to our ears. "I have weed," Peter's brother said, pulling out a small, transparent pouch. "I brought it from Kharagpur."

A Makeshift Bong

It was almost 1 AM, and the excitement in the room was palpable. But there was a problem.

"Do you guys have a bong or rolling paper?" he asked.

Samarth and I exchanged confused looks. We were too new to weed to even know what those were. Embarrassed, we admitted, "No, we don't."

Peter's brother laughed, unfazed. "No worries. I'll make a bong."

I was taken aback. "You can make a bong?" I asked, genuinely surprised.

"Of course," he replied, as though it were the simplest thing in the world. "We just need a few things: a pen, a small plastic bottle, and some aluminum foil."

Within minutes, we had gathered everything he needed from Peter's room—an Aladdin's cave of random items. Peter's room was like a Doraemon pocket; anything you needed could be found there.

Peter's brother worked with practiced efficiency. He removed the refill from the pen, heated a small metal object to make a hole in the middle of the bottle, and carefully inserted the pen. Next, he made another small hole in the bottle cap and covered it with aluminum foil, creating a makeshift bowl for the weed.

"We're almost done," he said, inspecting his work. "Now we just need some water."

We filled the bottle halfway, and the homemade bong was ready.

The First Encounter with Homemade Bong

As Peter's brother pulled out the weed from his pouch, my curiosity peaked. It looked nothing like I had imagined—small, dried leaves and stems that seemed more like something you'd find in a forest than the intoxicating substance I'd heard so much about.

"What are you doing now?" I asked as he started crushing the weed with his fingers.

"Removing the seeds and stems," he explained. "We only use the good stuff."

After meticulously preparing the weed, he asked, "Do you have a cigarette?"

I handed him one from the pack I had taken earlier. He roasted it with a lighter, explaining as he worked. "This makes it easier to mix the tobacco with the weed. It also makes the smoke smoother, so it doesn't burn your throat as much."

Once the mix was ready, he packed a small amount into the aluminum foil bowl on the bong. He turned to us with a grin. "Who's going first?"

"I'll do it," I said, my voice wavering slightly. I wasn't sure if it was excitement or nerves.

He sat me down, positioned the bong in front of me, and gave me simple instructions. "Place your mouth here and start sucking. I'll light the weed."

I followed his instructions, inhaling deeply as he lit the bowl. The smoke hit me hard—thick, bitter, and unlike anything I'd experienced. I coughed violently, my throat burning as my lungs struggled to keep up.

"You'll get used to it," he said, laughing. "Take a couple more hits."

I managed two more drags before handing the bong to the next person, my throat raw and my mind spinning. I excused myself and went back to my room, collapsing onto the bed. My thoughts raced, but my body felt heavy, pulling me into sleep before I could make sense of what I was feeling.

CHAPTER NINE

A MISFIT AMONG ACHIEVERS

Life was moving forward, but not in the way I had imagined. I wasn't attending classes anymore, just labs from 2 PM to 5 PM. Slowly, I realized something I couldn't deny—I wasn't good at studying anymore. It hit me hard every day, the regret of not going to school after 6th grade. I kept thinking about how big of a mistake that was. But there was nothing I could do now. I was in IIT, but the students around me were incredibly intelligent—not just in academics but in everything. They excelled at sports, cultural activities, and almost anything they tried. And then there was me, feeling lost and out of place.

I thought about my childhood a lot during these moments of self-reflection. Back then, I used to play cricket, and I was good at it too. I remember making a punching bag filled with sand so I could practice batting at home. People used to tell me I had talent. But I left cricket after 10th grade because I decided it wasn't a practical career choice. The odds of making it as a cricketer felt too slim, so I focused on studying instead. I thought playing cricket was a waste of time.

It wasn't just cricket I gave up. I had other interests too. I liked dancing, but I only ever danced at weddings. I liked singing, but my voice was so bad that whenever I tried to sing at home, people told me to shut up. So I started singing only when I was alone. Acting and action movies also fascinated me, but I never pursued them seriously. Sometimes, I'd grab my pillow, pretend it was a guitar, and sing my heart out. I enjoyed those moments, but they never went beyond the four walls of my room.

These thoughts played in my mind every day, especially when I saw people like Shaan and Shayan, the twin brothers in the CS department. They had All India Ranks below 100 in JEE Advanced. They weren't just academically brilliant—they were amazing at sports too. They played state-level table tennis, cricket, and badminton. Watching them reminded me of all the things I had given up, and it made me feel useless.

It wasn't just them. Most students here were like that—brilliant, multi-talented, and confident. And then there was me, struggling to keep up. These thoughts tore me apart. I couldn't focus on studying anymore. The exhaustion of constant comparison made me cry almost every night. I cried in silence, careful not to let my roommate hear me. I buried my face in a pillow to muffle the sound, trying to let it all out without anyone noticing. That was my routine—crying quietly every night—until I started going to EB37.

Things changed after I began visiting EB37 regularly. The crying stopped happening as often. I started vaping and smoking cigarettes, which helped me fall asleep faster. At least I wasn't crying myself to sleep every night anymore.

About ten days after my first bong-smoking experience, the midsem exams for the second semester began. There were four papers, and I was too busy during those days to think about anything else. But as soon as the exams ended, all my insecurities came rushing back. The students here were geniuses, and the professors designed questions that made me feel like I didn't belong. I was just a below-average guy in a sea of overachievers.

That evening, I went to EB37. Samarth was lying on his bed as usual, his MacBook resting on his chest, typing away. I sat down and asked him, "How were your exams?"

"Good," he replied casually, without much emotion.

He asked me the same question, and I lied, "Good." Deep down, I knew my performance was nowhere near good. I had just barely managed to write something on the paper, and I knew it wasn't enough. I stayed there, scrolling through my phone, trying to distract myself from my thoughts.

A little while later, Ayshu entered the room with his usual energy. "Bro, what are you guys doing? The midsem exams just ended—we should party!" he exclaimed.

That was the first time I had heard the word "party" used like this. At the time, I didn't think much of it. I left EB37 after a while and went back to my room to watch a movie. Around midnight, loud music started playing on the first floor. I immediately knew where it was coming from—EB37.

When I entered the room, it was completely dark. The only light came from Shaan's JBL speaker, which was blasting music. Ayshu was holding the speaker and dancing like he owned the floor. Watching him dance was an experience in itself—he weighed almost 100 kg, and his entire body, especially his chest, bounced with every move.

I couldn't help but laugh to myself. *Maybe that's why he turned off the lights—so no one could see his chest bouncing like that,* I thought.

I asked Shaan, "Is there anything to drink?"

He handed me a glass of vodka and said, "The juice is finished, so you'll have to drink it neat." I took a sip, the sharp taste burning my throat. I joined them on the dance floor, moving to the music, trying to blend in. But as I danced, I noticed something that stung—I was dancing alone. The others were paired off, laughing, enjoying themselves, and moving together. My insecurities crept back in. *Why doesn't anyone want to dance with me? What's wrong with me?*

As I stood there, feeling out of place, someone knocked on the door. Ayshu paused the music and called out, "Who is it?"

"It's me, Abheek," came the reply.

Hearing his name made me pause. Abheek was someone I didn't like much. He was good-looking, confident, and well-liked—everything I wasn't. I remembered an incident during Holi when I had accidentally broken his bucket. He'd confronted me about it later, but instead of admitting my mistake, I denied it. At the time, I felt like owning up would make me look weak. Looking back, I knew I had handled it poorly.

Abheek entered the room, and Ayshu greeted him warmly, offering him vodka and pulling out chips and juice from the cupboard. *Why doesn't anyone treat me like this?* I thought bitterly.

Trying to break the awkwardness, I leaned toward Abheek and said, "I want to debate."

He looked surprised but smiled. "Sure, I can help you," he said.

"But my English isn't good," I admitted.

"No problem," he replied. "You can debate in Hindi."

His response was kind, but I didn't feel any better. I left the room shortly after, realizing I wasn't enjoying myself. The vodka wasn't working on me anymore, and my insecurities were louder than the music. Back in my room, I lay on my bed, staring at the ceiling, my thoughts spiraling. I hated feeling like I didn't belong. Sleep didn't come easy that night.

CHAPTER TEN

THE FIRST YEAR'S END

The end of the first year felt like a culmination of everything I had been through and yet, paradoxically, nothing at all. The months had passed in a blur, one moment rushing into the next, and now, here I was—packing my bags, getting ready to head back home for the two-month holiday. My roommate, who had been with me through it all, had already left, his side of the room empty and untouched. The silence was louder than anything else.

As I stuffed clothes into my trolley, I found myself thinking about him. He didn't like me, not really. He was polite, but there was always a wall between us. He was someone who excelled at academics. Every exam, every test, he topped. And there was me, the one who struggled to even show up to lectures, the one who studied the night before just to scrape through. Somehow, by God's grace, I passed everything. But there was always that nagging feeling that I wasn't enough.

I missed him, in a way. He wasn't the most affectionate person, but he was a good listener. Every time I needed to talk about something, whether it was about my day or my rambling thoughts about life, he'd listen. He never judged, never interrupted. He just listened. And in my world of chaos and confusion, that meant a lot more than I realized at the time.

I remembered the night of January 1st, when I'd come back to the room drunk after the party. He had been furious. I could see the anger in his eyes as he called Aaryan Oganja, a senior, to tell him that I was drunk and he didn't want me in the room. Aaryan's reply was simple: "Is he disturbing you?" he'd asked. "No," my roommate had said, and Aaryan told him to call him when I started causing problems.

That was the moment I felt like I wasn't doing something completely wrong. In my drunken state, I had thought I was being an idiot, but in that moment, I realized that I wasn't. My roommate didn't like me, but he didn't want me to get into trouble either. There was a strange, silent respect between us. It wasn't friendship, not exactly, but it was something. And it had been enough to keep us going through the year.

As I zipped up my trolley bag, I looked around the room one last time. It seemed completely empty, and yet I could still feel the echoes of everything that had happened here. The walls, the bed, the desk—all of it was a part of the story that had unfolded over the past seven months. Seven months. It felt like just seven days. Time had slipped away, and now it was over. I was about to leave this room behind, and with it, a chapter of my life that I wasn't sure I was ready to close.

I moved to EB37, the unofficial hangout spot that had seen so many late nights, conversations, and shared experiences. The room was completely messy, just as I had left it. Everyone had already left, but the trash was still there, scattered across the floor like the remnants of forgotten stories. There was one thing that stood out—the name "Syra" written on the wall in ashes from the countless cigarettes I had smoked.

I stared at it for a long time. I had written her name so many times, with each cigarette, each moment of loneliness, each fleeting thought of what could have been. I still remembered the first time I saw her—the way she looked, the way she carried herself. I had spent so much of my first semester trying to capture that image, to make sense of it. I used to drink so I could see her clearly in my vision, to imagine her presence in my life. I used to walk from one room to another, telling anyone who would listen about how beautiful she was, how different she felt from everyone else.

But that was me back then—lost, confused, and desperate to feel something, anything. Maybe that was one of the reasons people started calling me "nashedi." They thought I was just another college kid using substances to escape, to numb the reality of being at IIT, of not feeling like I belonged. And in many ways, they were right.

I pulled out a cigarette from my pocket and lit it. The smoke curled around me, and I inhaled deeply. My mind wandered back to Syra. It had been seven months, and I still hadn't forgotten her. I wondered if I ever would. She had become an obsession, a symbol of everything I hadn't been able to express. But in this moment, with the smoke filling my lungs and the flickering light of the room around me, I knew that this was the end of it. I was leaving this space behind, and I would leave the memories of Syra and my old habits with it.

I smoked in silence, lost in thought, until the cigarette burned down to its last ember. I turned the cigarette in my fingers, watching as the ash fell away. The name "Syra" I had written on the wall—now reduced to nothing but burnt remnants—was like a symbol of the past I was about to leave behind. I was cutting ties with the old me, the one who relied on substances and distractions to deal with life.

I crushed the cigarette in my hand, and for the first time in a long while, I felt something shift inside me. I didn't know what was next, but I knew that the next semester would be different. I was going to stop drinking, stop smoking, and stop obsessing over things I couldn't control. I was going to focus on what mattered—the reason I was here at IIT. I had to do it. There was no turning back now.

As I made my way out of EB37, the weight of the year pressed down on me. It hadn't been easy. In fact, it had been harder than anything I had ever done. The constant comparison to others, the pressure to perform, the self-doubt—it had all been overwhelming. But in this moment, I realized that I had made it through. I had survived the first year, and I was leaving behind a version of myself that was broken, unsure, and full of empty promises.

I had learned a lot. Not just about academics, but about who I was and who I could become. It was a process, and it wasn't going to happen overnight. But the first step was realizing that I could change.

I thought about my father, who had always supported me financially. I had promised myself that by the end of my first year, I would be financially independent. I wouldn't rely on him anymore for college fees or personal expenses. But here I was, at the end of my first year, and I hadn't done anything towards that goal. I hadn't even figured out what I wanted to do with my life. The weight of that realization hit me hard, but it was a necessary truth. I couldn't keep avoiding it.

I walked back to my room, the empty room where the echoes of the past year still lingered. It felt strange to think that this chapter was ending. I had spent so much time trying to escape reality, trying to numb myself with distractions. But now, I had no choice but to face what was ahead.

The first year was over, and it had been a whirlwind. But as I closed the door behind me for the last time, I knew that I was ready for what was next. I didn't know exactly what it would be, but I was going to start living with purpose. I was going to stop running.

THE UNEXPECTED TRIO

Time passed, and it was the beginning of my second year. The campus had changed, but so had I. I was now a second-year student, a "senior" by college standards, but honestly, I didn't feel like one. The familiar faces had started to blur, and the new batch of first-year students seemed even more energetic and sharp than I ever was. But in my own little bubble, things felt steady—at least for now.

I was back in my hostel, and this time, the room arrangement was different. The college usually gave us triple-shared rooms, but somehow, I had ended up sharing the space with Samarth and Anmol Tiwari. An unlikely combination—at least to me. Samarth was still the same. Always the one trying to lead, whether it was deciding where to buy alcohol or figuring out the best party plans. He had this uncanny ability to take charge of any situation, though he always managed to fail in the end. But despite that, I respected him. He was the one person who truly understood me, or at least that's what I convinced myself of.

Anmol, on the other hand, was a bit of a mystery. He wasn't part of the cool crowd; in fact, he was pretty much the opposite. He was the kind of guy who laughed at every bad joke, smiled awkwardly in social situations, and never really contributed much to the conversation. He wasn't unfriendly, but he was certainly unremarkable. He was the kind of person who blended into the background like a pot in a room. And yet, somehow, we had ended up together. Samarth, Anmol, and me. The trio that seemed so odd at first glance but somehow clicked together over time.

We had our own little system. Samarth and I shared a bed to maximize space, leaving Anmol with the other side of the room. Our little corner of the hostel was often a chaotic mix of sounds—people coming in and out, music playing, and random banter that made the space feel alive. This was the start of a new semester, the end of July, and the beginning of a fresh start for me. I came back with a new energy, determined to make the most of my second year. I woke up earlier, started taking baths regularly, and actually attended classes. It felt good—this was how life was supposed to be, right? I'd be different this time.

But as always, that initial burst of energy didn't last long. After two weeks of regular attendance and feeling like I was on top of my game, I fell back into the familiar rhythm of skipping classes, sleeping until noon, and avoiding work. The guilt that crept in with each skipped class was easily drowned by distractions: my phone, friends, and whatever else I could find to keep me from confronting the fact that I was still slacking off. Old habits die hard.

Around this time, I met Om. He was from our hostel, but we had never really spoken in the first year. He lived next door to me, but we barely exchanged more than a few words. I knew he was the kind of person who didn't drink or smoke, which, in our hostel culture, made him an anomaly. But he was also a genuinely nice guy—always helping people out without asking for anything in return.

I remember a time during the first year, when I was sick, that Om had stepped in to help me. He had an electric kettle in his room, and he used it to warm water for me when I couldn't even muster the energy to go to the mess. I still remembered the kindness he showed me when I was feeling down, and even though we didn't talk much, I respected him for that.

Then, there was the time during the college fest. SAC (Student Activity Center) was the heart of all the fest-related activity, and there were always tons of leftover supplies after the event. Om, being the resourceful guy he was, heard about the stockpile of water bottles in one of the rooms at SAC. Without a second thought, he grabbed a few of his friends, snuck into the room, and wrapped up as many water bottles as he could find in his t-shirt, hauling them back to the hostel. He didn't just keep the bottles for himself; he shared them with everyone in the hostel, even gave me one. That small act of kindness was something I hadn't forgotten.

By the time third semester rolled around, Om had become my lab partner. We had nearly every class together—whether it was labs, lectures, or assignments. It was funny how things worked out, because suddenly, we were not just hostel mates, but wing mates, college mates, class mates, and lab mates all rolled into one. Initially, we didn't talk much. Our conversations were mostly limited to work-related topics. He'd knock on my door in the mornings to wake me up and drag me to class or labs. I wasn't always the best at sticking to schedules, so I appreciated his punctuality.

Our room had slowly evolved into the unofficial hangout spot of the hostel. Samarth, who always found a way to bring people together (even if his leadership attempts were often comically bad), had created a magnetic pull around our space. People started drifting in and out, bringing their own energy to the room. It wasn't just about hanging out anymore; it was about a sense of belonging, a feeling of being part of something bigger. And I couldn't help but feel grateful for that.

But things weren't always perfect. My mind would often wander, and I'd catch myself slipping back into that familiar feeling of inadequacy. I started to wonder if I had truly changed. Was I still the person I had been before? The one who lacked direction, who was content to float through life? And then there was Syra. It had been over a year, but I still couldn't shake the image of her from my mind. She was a ghost in my thoughts, haunting me even as I tried to focus on my studies or my friendships.

I realized that I hadn't fully let go of the past, and that uncertainty was starting to show in my actions. Despite the progress I thought I was making, I was still unsure of what I really wanted to do with my life. The sense of belonging I felt with Samarth, Om, and the others gave me comfort, but it was also a reminder that I was still searching for something.

For now, life at college seemed to be moving forward at its own pace. I was surrounded by people who, in their own way, helped me feel less alone. But I knew that deep down, I still had a long way to go before I could truly understand who I was and what I wanted out of all of this.

CHAPTER TWELVE

A NEW PERSONA

By now, I had become close to a select group of people—Samarth, Anmol, and Om—each of whom had their own way of living, their own philosophies. Samarth lived life on his own terms: study for a day before exams and then party for the rest of the semester, often topping everything with ease. Om was more methodical: he went to class, studied, and stayed on top of things without ever looking for an excuse. Anmol was in the middle, unsure about where life was taking him. And then there was me, somewhere in between, trying to figure out how to strike a balance between Samarth's carefree spirit and Om's disciplined approach.

But one thing was for sure: life wasn't as dull anymore. I had started carving out my space, finding my identity in the chaos of hostel life, and I owed some of that to Samarth.

It all started with a simple gesture. Samarth's brother came back from the US for a visit. He was the kind of guy everyone admired—cool, carefree, and full of stories. And when he arrived, he brought with him three bottles of Absolut vodka and a huge pack of cigarettes—12 packs to be precise. I couldn't believe it. I was just staring at the bottles, and I remember saying to Samarth, "Bro, what the hell? Your brother is so cool! I want to be like him when I grow up."

Samarth laughed it off. He didn't seem phased by it, but to me, it was an entire shift in how I saw him and, somehow, how I saw myself. Here was this guy who didn't care about rules and boundaries, who was living life on his own terms—and for the first time in a while, I wanted a piece of that.

He handed me one of the cigarette packs, and I, being the guy who never really got hooked to smoking, figured, "Why not?" I wasn't addicted to smoking yet, but after a few smokes, I started to notice the changes in my behavior.

Slowly, my room became the hangout spot for the entire wing. It was like I had become the unofficial supplier, the go-to guy for cigarettes. It was kind of a funny feeling—people would come, hang around, and I would just provide the cigarettes. I didn't know why, but it felt like I had a little more power now. A little more influence. The best part? I didn't even need to initiate the conversation. They did it for me. It felt almost effortless—just a quick "Got a cigarette?" and then they would sit down, and we'd talk. I had this strange sense of authority now, the guy who everyone came to for a smoke, the guy who had something to offer.

It wasn't just about the cigarettes though. It was about what happened when people came over. I started listening. And it felt good to be heard, to be part of something that wasn't just about me.

Let me introduce you to some of the people who started becoming regulars in my life. There was Adheer, a towering 6'5" basketball player, quiet unless cigarettes were involved. At first, he didn't talk much. But soon, he became a fixture in our group, talking about basketball, about his life. He didn't need to say much to make his presence known.

Then, there was Peter. He didn't speak much either but always laughed at my bad jokes. He was the kind of guy who was always kind to everyone, doing whatever people asked of him. But for the most part, he'd be glued to his laptop, playing FIFA day and night, barely attending classes or labs.

Rayaan Panda was another one in our wing. People used to make fun of him a lot, mostly because of his tendency to act like he was constantly "down." But he was the guy you'd go to if you were feeling low. His antics were so ridiculous that you couldn't help but laugh, no matter how bad your day had been.

Then, there was Shantanu. Tall, thin, and awkward, with no muscle on his body. But he was one of the most unpredictable guys in the group. You never knew what he was going to say or when, and half the time, it didn't make any sense. Still, his randomness brought an odd charm to the group.

Finally, there was Ayshu. A chubby guy who couldn't stop talking. And when I say talking, I mean *talking*. Non-stop. I didn't like him much because I felt his jokes were forced, fake even. He'd crack jokes in front of everyone, but personally, I never found them funny. Yet, people would laugh because of the way he said it—his enthusiasm was infectious, even if the joke wasn't.

This was my group now. The group that revolved around cigarettes, and I was at the center of it. At first, it felt strange—like I had slipped into a role I didn't know I wanted. But soon, I started noticing that I was becoming one of them, blending into their personalities and habits. I was no longer the silent observer in the corner. I was part of the chain, a link that held everything together.

People started asking me questions, engaging with me about life, about their own stories. And I listened. I wasn't used to this before—people seeking me out to share their lives. It felt good, like I had finally found my place in this world. There was no more loneliness. The isolation I had felt in the past—being an outsider, always comparing myself to others—was slowly dissolving. People respected me. And that respect wasn't because I was special or had done anything extraordinary. It was simply because I had cigarettes to offer. But that small action, that little bit of authority, shifted how I was viewed. It made me feel like I mattered.

I started to understand something about myself, something I hadn't realized before. When people look up to you, even for something as trivial as cigarettes, it changes your perspective. I wasn't just some guy in the corner anymore. I was someone people went to. I started to see that respect isn't always earned through grand gestures, but sometimes, just through small acts of kindness—offering a cigarette, listening to someone's problems, or just being there when people needed you.

As the days passed, I started feeling better about who I was and where I was headed. For the first time in a long time, I wasn't drowning in my insecurities. I was becoming part of something bigger than myself. My loneliness was fading. I had a group now, people who cared about me, even if it was just for a smoke. And maybe, just maybe, that was all I needed to start moving forward.

CHAPTER THIRTEEN

THE FIRST TASTE OF ESCAPISM

The thing about cigarettes is that they don't last forever. And the moment Samarth's brother's stash of cigarettes ran out, I began to wonder if people would stop coming to me. After all, I had no more to offer. But to my surprise, they didn't stop. They still came, not for the cigarettes anymore, but for me, or maybe for what I had become. The cigarettes were just a pretext to gather, but something bigger was happening, something deeper. I didn't realize it yet, but I was starting to become the center of something.

And then, Samarth brought something else.

It was a day like any other when he walked into the room with a small bag, and without even a second thought, he asked me, "Bro, will you smoke weed?" I didn't know what to say at first, so I just shrugged and said, "Why not?" It was strange to think about; this was a whole new level, something I hadn't ever done before. When I asked Samarth where he got it from, he casually replied, "I scored it."

That's when I learned what "scored" meant in the context of weed. It meant he bought it directly from a dealer. This was a whole new world opening up in front of me, and like most things in my life, I wasn't sure whether I should dive in or just stay on the edge and watch. But, in that moment, I felt an odd curiosity, the same feeling I got when I first smoked cigarettes.

The room was just me, Samarth, and Anmol. We closed the door, as our room had officially turned into the unofficial hangout spot. It felt strange, but there was a sense of pleasure in knowing people were drawn to me, that my room was where the action was. Samarth started teaching me how to crush the weed, showing me how to remove the stems and seeds. I didn't quite understand it at first, but after 15 minutes of focused effort, we finally had the weed ready. Anmol, as usual, was sitting in the corner, his earbuds firmly in place, not paying attention to us unless he had to.

Samarth then pulled out a cigarette, unwrapped it, and began mixing the tobacco with the weed. I watched as he skillfully used a rolling paper to make a joint. The process was methodical: filling the paper with a small plastic pipe, pressing the weed in, rolling it tight, and sealing it with a swift twist of the paper. It was fascinating, like watching a magician at work. The whole thing felt like a rite of passage—something I never thought I'd be a part of.

Finally, Samarth lit the joint, and we passed it around, each of us taking a long drag. We smoked it down to the end, and the high hit me slowly. I could feel my body sink into the bed, the room spinning just a little, the air thick with smoke. It was a surreal feeling, like I was floating in space, disconnected from everything around me. We sat on the bed in silence for a few minutes, just absorbing the feeling of being high.

Then, Anmol broke the silence. "Remember that day when we smoked for the first time?" he asked, his voice far away, like he was lost in a memory. Samarth and I nodded, recalling the moment.

That day was unforgettable, a blur of smoke, laughter, and confusion. It was one of those moments when everything seems so much clearer—until the reality of the situation sets in. We had been sitting in the room, five of us, listening to music. Samarth had his guitar, and we were all chatting aimlessly when suddenly, I picked up the guitar and pretended to play. But something strange happened. Anmol, who had been staring at me, looked up and said, "Bro, what the fuck? You actually play the guitar well!"

I remember thinking, "Wait, I'm not even playing!" But in that haze, none of us could tell the difference. We were so high that we all started to believe the song playing from the speaker was actually coming from my fingers on the guitar. It felt like the guitar was alive, like the music had become a part of us. We laughed at how ridiculous the situation was, but at the same time, it felt so real, so true. We were lost in the moment, and it was the first time I felt truly, completely out of touch with everything around me.

We sat there, talking and laughing, caught in a haze of confusion and euphoria, wondering if the line between reality and fantasy had blurred forever. Maybe it didn't matter. We were high, and in that moment, that was enough. The world outside our room didn't exist. We didn't need it.

It was strange, though—after that experience, I started to feel something shift inside me. I wasn't sure what it was yet, but something was changing. Maybe it was the weed, or maybe it was the way my life was unfolding. Either way, the more I smoked, the more I felt like I was becoming someone else, someone I didn't fully recognize but was growing comfortable with.

FINDING CONFIDENCE IN THE HAZE

Samarth had officially become the plug. Weed was now a staple in our lives. He started scoring regularly, and that meant I had full-time access to it. It wasn't long before smoking weed became a ritual for us—a consistent escape every two or three days. Anmol, who initially seemed indifferent about everything, developed an attachment to the after-effects of smoking. He felt like it gave him a new sense of confidence, especially when roaming around campus.

After a smoke session, Anmol would bolt out of the room with one mission in mind: to roam the campus and, in his words, "rizz up" girls. It was amusing to watch him. He genuinely believed that his newfound confidence from weed would help him find a girlfriend. Samarth and I didn't share the same level of ambition. For us, the late-night campus walks were just about enjoying the trip, making fun of whoever crossed our path, and soaking in the strange, euphoric calm of the night.

Our campus was vast and mysterious at night, with its dimly lit pathways and pockets of darkness where couples would steal private moments. The main building was about a kilometer away from our hostel, and even at 2 a.m., it would buzz with clusters of boys and girls hanging out. Walking there in our altered state felt like an adventure, a playground where inhibitions didn't exist.

The New Me Emerging

It was during these weed-fueled nights that I began noticing a change in myself. The insecurities that had chained me for so long, the overthinking that kept me up at night, the fear of failure and judgment—all of it faded away. After smoking, I felt lighter, clearer. It wasn't just the high; it was a version of me I hadn't met in years, possibly ever.

One night, after a session, I randomly barged into Abheek's room. Abheek, as you might remember, was the debating representative of our hostel. Something inside me compelled me to ask him for a topic to debate. At first, he looked at me like I'd lost my mind, but then he smiled and threw a topic at me. I don't even remember what it was, but I debated fiercely, letting my thoughts flow without overthinking.

For the first time, I realized I had a voice. My thoughts, experiences, and opinions had value, and I could articulate them well when I wasn't bogged down by my internal fears. I knew this wasn't just the weed talking; it was me, the real me, finally breaking through the years of self-doubt and isolation.

Abheek seemed impressed, and a few days later, he organized a friendly debate in the hostel. There were about ten participants, and we were divided into teams. I was paired with a guy named Arnav Singal, while Samarth and another boy, Anurag Kumar, formed the opposing team. The topic was "Long-term relationship is better than short-term relationships." My team had to argue in favor of long-term relationship.

I still remember the intensity of that debate. I spoke with confidence and clarity, countering every point made by Samarth and Anurag Kumar. It felt surreal—like I was finally tapping into a part of myself that had been buried under years of silence. When the debate ended, I had single-handedly won it for my team.

For the first time in years, I felt proud of myself. It wasn't about beating Samarth, though that did feel good, especially since I had always looked up to him as someone naturally charismatic. It was about proving to myself that I could shine, that I wasn't just the shadow of the people around me.

The Spiral

This newfound confidence was intoxicating. I started walking differently, carrying myself with the same ease I had back in school when life was simpler, before the pressure of JEE preparation and the loneliness that followed had weighed me down. Weed became a regular part of my nights, not just with Anmol and Samarth but with others from our wing—Peter, Shantanu, devansh, Adheer. Every night, we'd gather, smoke, and talk until 2 or 3 a.m.

But somewhere deep inside, I couldn't shake the feeling that it wasn't enough. The laughter, the camaraderie, the confidence—it felt real in the moment, but in the quiet hours after everyone had left, a gnawing emptiness would creep back in.

I started questioning myself. Was this the real me, or was I just hiding behind the haze? Was this confidence mine, or was it the weed speaking for me? And these friendships—were they genuine, or were they built on the thin foundation of shared highs and stolen cigarettes?

No matter how much I tried to push these thoughts away, they lingered. I began to feel like I was living two lives: the confident, carefree version of myself that existed in the smoke-filled nights and the uncertain, searching version that emerged when the high wore off.

A Growing Divide

Even as I grew closer to the people around me, a part of me remained detached. I was torn between embracing this new social circle and yearning for something more substantial, something that felt authentic.

The weed sessions continued, the debates came and went, and I kept moving forward, but the feeling that it wasn't enough wouldn't go away. I was changing, yes, but I wasn't sure if I was becoming the person I wanted to be or just a version of myself shaped by my surroundings.

CHAPTER FIFTEEN

THE RISHIKESH TRIP – A WEED - FUELED ESCAPE

It was around 10 PM, the night after our mid-sem exams, and we were all hanging out in our usual spot—high and vibing as the weed session was in full swing. We were a mix of tired, excited, and completely zoned out. That's when Samarth, ever the instigator, threw out the wildest suggestion.

"Let's go on a trip," he said, like it was the most natural thing in the world.

Shantanu, who had been quietly sitting on the floor, looked up and asked, "Where to?"

"Rishikesh," Ayshu chimed in, clearly enjoying the randomness of it all.

I didn't even hesitate. "Okay."

Anmol, as usual, didn't care about much, so he just nodded and said, "Yeah, why not."

And then, there was Malik. You know the type—the guy who doesn't smoke, doesn't drink, but somehow always ends up with us in these spontaneous adventures. We call him Malik, and he's one of those people who could sit with us while we passed the joint, and he'd happily crush it for us. He didn't want to feel left out, but once he started talking, you couldn't get him to stop. He was this ball of energy, and honestly, the guy never had a shortage of words. Ever.

Malik's voice rang out, "I'm in!"

And just like that, we were ready to go.

We had no plan, no idea what we were doing, but that's the magic of weed—it makes everything feel like a great idea. We didn't waste a second. Everyone scrambled back to their rooms in a flurry, grabbed a college bag and some clothes, and before you knew it, we had booked a cab. This all happened in about ten minutes.

The whole gang was there: Malik, Shantanu, Samarth, Anmol, Devansh, Pratyaksh, and me. All seven of us piled into the cab. I was sitting in the front seat, the victory seat—I'd won a race against everyone just to claim it. Honestly, at that point, I was so high I didn't even know what I was doing. But I was excited. This was going to be an adventure.

The drive to the bus stand felt like a blur. By the time we were on the bus to Rishikesh, I wasn't really conscious of much. Time passed quickly—too quickly, actually. And that's when I learned an important lesson: if you're high enough, even a long journey feels like it lasts five minutes.

Somehow, I ended up in Rishikesh. I still don't remember how we got there. But the memory of the trip is burned into my mind. And here's something else I realized: if you're high enough, the journey doesn't feel as long as it really is. Time and space just warp around you.

The Search for Weed in Rishikesh

Once we arrived, Samarth, always the leader—even if his leadership skills were questionable—took charge and started leading us through the streets. But there was one little problem. We were out of weed. And in a place like Rishikesh, weed wasn't exactly sold at every corner shop.

So, Samarth, not one to back down from a challenge, started asking the locals. He went up to a rickshaw driver and asked, "Do you know where I can get weed?"

The guy didn't understand at first and then flat out refused.

"No, no, no!" he waved his hands.

Undeterred, Samarth went to a couple of shopkeepers, repeating the same question. But each one turned him down, giving us confused looks as if Samarth had just asked them for the moon. We were all watching this unfold, laughing like it was the funniest thing ever. It wasn't so much the failure as it was Samarth's complete inability to stop. Every rejection made him more determined, like some bizarre treasure hunt for the elusive green.

Eventually, we gave up on the search and continued with our trip, laughing and joking the whole time. But it wasn't just the laughter; it was a sense of freedom that hung in the air. We were away from campus, from classes, from everything.

The Ganga Bath

One of the things I'd always wanted to do in Rishikesh was bathe in the Ganga. It wasn't just for the experience—it was for what I believed it symbolized. I had heard people say that if you take a dip in the holy river, all your past sins would be washed away. It was a deeply spiritual thought for me, and in my mind, it felt like the perfect way to reset everything.

So, I went into the Ganga. The cold water hit me like a shock. But when I stepped out, I didn't feel any different. It wasn't like weed, where you instantly feel something kick in. The moment passed, and I just stood there, dripping wet, realizing that it didn't work the way I had imagined. The sins, the past, the baggage—it didn't vanish.

It was a strange feeling—disappointment mixed with a bit of realization. Maybe there wasn't an easy way to wash away the past. Maybe it wasn't that simple. I didn't know, but I had expected something bigger.

The Ride Back – A Roasting Turned on Me

The trip back to the hostel was a different kind of trip altogether. I was sitting at the front of the bus, as usual, alone with my thoughts. Behind me, Ayshu and Shantanu were talking and joking around. Ayshu, being himself, started roasting me—making fun of me like he always did. His humor was always a little too sharp, a little too cutting. But something inside me snapped.

I had enough.

I'd been the butt of his jokes for so long, laughing it off, trying not to let it bother me. But tonight, maybe it was the weed, maybe it was the vibe, but I wasn't going to let him get away with it anymore. Without thinking, I turned around and started roasting him back. Hard.

And man, it felt good.

I didn't just stop at his usual jabs. I hit him with everything I had, making fun of him in front of Shantanu, who was sitting there, wide-eyed, watching in shock.

Ayshu, for once, didn't have a comeback. He just put his head down, silent.

And that's when I realized: I'd just roasted the guy who always roasts everyone. The guy who never showed an ounce of anger, the one who always played the joker. I had flipped the script, and it felt so damn satisfying.

But as I sat back in my seat, the high starting to wear off, I wondered, *What the hell just happened?* Had I really just lost it like that? Had the weed made me snap?

It wasn't like me. I never really got angry. I was never the type to lash out. So why had I done it? Was it the weed? Or was it something deeper—something about how I had been feeling lately? The confusion lingered as I stared out the window, the landscape passing by, lost in my thoughts.

The Aftermath

The whole trip felt like a haze—a blur of good times, new experiences, and, oddly enough, self-discovery. We laughed, we joked, we had fun, but somewhere beneath it all, I was starting to feel the weight of something. I didn't know what it was, but the high was starting to wear off, and with it, the sense of euphoria began to fade. In its place was a quiet realization: maybe I had been running from something. Maybe I wasn't really escaping at all.

As the bus rolled back into the hostel, I couldn't help but wonder if I had actually learned something. Or if I was just numbing myself. But that night, one thing was clear—I had changed. And whatever that change was, I wasn't sure I was ready for it.

CHAPTER SIXTEEN

THE DOUBLE – EDGED SWORD

After the trip to Rishikesh, something inside me had shifted. I wasn't the same person anymore. In fact, I didn't even recognize the person I was becoming. It felt like I had stepped into a new world, one where humor and roasting were my weapons, my way of connecting with others, and strangely, even a way to feel powerful.

I started making fun of people—targeting anyone I could. Initially, it felt weird. I had never been the type to roast anyone before. In fact, growing up, I was the quiet guy who just took everything in, listening to taunts and jokes without ever replying. I was always the one who overthought every interaction, every word, every gesture. But now, after that trip, something inside me snapped. I realized that the key to socializing, to fitting in, to gaining respect wasn't just about being nice or agreeable. No, it was about the jokes, the one-liners, the quick comebacks. It was about how much laughter you could pull out of a group.

I remembered my friend Priyanshu(PDS), who had always been quick with his words, always making jokes, roasting people left and right. And Abheek, who could roast anyone in the most brutal, yet funny way, always leaving the person laughing even if they were the victim. I had always admired their confidence—their ability to speak without hesitation, to make anyone laugh, to take control of a conversation.

So, I thought, why not? I could do that too. Maybe it was time for me to stop being the quiet guy and start becoming someone who could stand up for himself and, more importantly, stand out.

It wasn't long before I found my target: Rayaan Panda. Rayaan was one of those people who never really stood out—he was quiet, a bit awkward, but not a bad guy. The perfect target. The first few roasts were weak, nothing impressive. I didn't have the quick wit that Samarth or Abheek had, but I kept going. Slowly, I got better. I started to study the reactions of the group—how they laughed, how they looked at me. The more they laughed, the more I enjoyed it.

Something clicked. It wasn't just about making fun of Rayaan anymore; it was about feeling *alive*. I felt in control, in a way that I hadn't before. People laughed, I laughed, and for once, I wasn't just sitting in the background, feeling small and invisible. No, I was at the center of it all. I had found my power.

But here's the thing about roasting—it's a double-edged sword. I had learned that if you roast someone, you make yourself vulnerable to the same treatment. If you dish it out, you better be ready to take it too. And that scared me.

I started noticing a shift. I had become that guy—the one who roasted people, made fun of them, made everyone laugh. But deep down, I started wondering if this was really me or just a persona I had created. I began to question: What if people started targeting me the same way I was targeting others? What if my jokes, my comebacks, came back to bite me? That thought lingered in the back of my mind, creeping in at night when the laughter faded and I was alone with my thoughts.

I realized I needed a strategy. This new persona I had adopted was fun, but I couldn't risk being seen as the guy who only knows how to roast. I didn't want to end up the target myself. So, I went to the person who I knew could give me some solid advice—Abheek. He was like a mentor to me.

I asked him about my fear—what happens if I roast someone and they turn on me? What if they roast me back and I'm left speechless? His response was simple but powerful: "It's a normal thing, bro. I went through it too."

I was shocked. The idea that even someone like Abheek, who seemed to have everything figured out, had been in the same place as me was a revelation. He went on to explain that after you roast someone, you just have to talk to them like a normal person afterward. Be nice. Be real. You don't have to stay in the "roast mode" forever. Just show respect, and they'll respect you back.

It was a simple concept, but it made so much sense. I had been approaching this whole thing wrong. I wasn't supposed to be this aggressive, constant source of humor. No, I could have fun with people, roast them, make everyone laugh, but then I had to let it go. I had to show that I could be a friend, a genuine person too. That was how I could protect myself and still maintain respect in the group.

So, I started doing just that. First, I'd roast someone—lighthearted, funny, not mean-spirited. Then, after a day or two, I'd talk to them like nothing had happened. Slowly, I was getting better at balancing it. The key was to make people laugh without crossing the line, to roast without making anyone feel bad. And you know what?

It worked. People respected me more, and the friendships I was building were stronger.

But still, a part of me didn't like the idea of talking behind people's backs. I couldn't get into the habit of bitching about people when they weren't around. It felt wrong, fake. There was a war inside me—on one side, I had this new, confident, social version of myself, the guy who could roast and command attention. On the other side, I had the old me, the guy who hated conflict, who preferred peace over drama, who couldn't stand when things got too real or harsh.

I had found myself in a strange place—caught between two versions of me. The old, quiet guy who would never talk back and the new, confident guy who felt alive with every roast.

But the truth was, I didn't know who I was anymore. Was I the guy who made people laugh, or was I just playing a part to avoid my real feelings? The more I roasted, the more I laughed, the more I started to question: *Was I becoming the villain or the hero of my own story?*

I didn't have the answers yet, but the search for them had begun. Every joke, every laugh, every sharp comeback pushed me closer to discovering who I really was—and whether or not I liked who I was becoming.

CHAPTER SEVENTEEN

BREAKING THE CAGE – THE SOLO FLIGHT

I started to feel the conflict brewing inside me. For five years, I had lived alone—trapped in my own world, disconnected from the outside. But now, just one year into IIT, everything was changing. I was different. The person I was becoming was in sharp contrast to the one I had been. I wasn't sure who I was anymore. Was I the lonely, content person who had learned to live with solitude? Or was I someone else, someone who craved the company of others, surrounded by friends, laughter, and noise?

I couldn't decide. It felt like I was stuck between two versions of myself, each pulling me in different directions. And just when I thought I might never figure it out, the college holidays arrived. And with it, an opportunity I had been waiting for—a chance to go on a solo trip.

I had always wanted to travel alone. A trip where I didn't have to answer to anyone, where I didn't need to fit into anyone else's plans. I wanted to know if I could truly enjoy being on my own, or if I was better suited to the company of others.

A month earlier, I had gone on a trip to Rishikesh with my friends. The laughter, the conversations, the moments of carefree joy—it had been amazing. But now, I needed to do something different. I needed to figure out who I really was, and this solo trip was the perfect way to find out.

My cousin, who was studying in Dehradun, had always been a steady presence in my life. I called her up and told her about my plan. "I'm thinking of going to Mussoorie alone," I said. "That sounds amazing!" she replied. "I can send you all the details for a cab and a good guide there." She sent me the information I needed, and just like that, everything fell into place.

I told Samarth about my plan, and though he didn't believe me at first, he handed me a joint to take along for the ride. "Going solo, huh?" he said with a grin, clearly surprised. "Well, enjoy." I could see he was skeptical, but he had no idea how serious I was.

It was around 5 p.m. in mid-October when I started packing. I moved fast—no time to second-guess. I grabbed my things, threw them into my bag, and lit the joint right before leaving the hostel. The weed took over me, filling me with a sense of confidence I had never known before. I was about to embark on a 300-km journey, 1000 km away from home, with no one to hold my hand. I felt a kind of liberation that I couldn't explain.

I was 19 years old, and this was my moment to break free. To leave behind the walls I had built around myself. The walls I had lived within for so long. No one knew I was leaving. My parents didn't know. This was my decision, my journey.

I made my way to the bus stand, feeling a mix of excitement and uncertainty. I wasn't scared, though. I was high, sure, but I was also ready. I felt lighter than ever. I found a bus to Dehradun and climbed on, sat by the window, and let my mind wander. I began thinking about the last trip to Rishikesh—how easy it had been to laugh and talk with friends. But now, here I was, sitting alone, looking out at the world through the window. It was different. But it wasn't lonely.

And that's when it hit me. I wasn't alone. I had never really been alone. The person I had been, the person who spent five years locked in isolation, had built walls so high around himself that he couldn't see beyond them. For so long, I had been that bird trapped in a cage, dreaming of flying but too scared to leave.

And now, here I was, on a bus to Mussoorie. A year ago, this would have been unimaginable. I had spent five years trapped in my own thoughts, not moving, not living. But now, the walls were falling. The cage was breaking.

I realized that I had spent years in the cage of my own making, afraid of the world outside. I had built a world within my head, where everything was safe, quiet, and predictable. But I had also been trapped in that world. It was like a bird dreaming of the sky, but never able to spread its wings.

The weed, the journey, the new experiences—this was all breaking me free. Slowly but surely, the cage I had built around myself, brick by brick, was crumbling. It was like I had been given wings, and for the first time in my life, I was soaring.

I thought about the years I had spent in isolation. At home, I never went out, never did anything for myself. I was always with my parents, always surrounded by the same routine. A trip like this would have been unthinkable just a year ago. But now? I was doing it. I was living the life I had always dreamed of, the life I had imagined while staring out at the world through my cage bars.

I reached Dehradun around 2 a.m. I called my sister to let her know I had arrived. She didn't know I was alone. She thought I was with friends. "How many people are with you?" she asked. I lied and said, "Four." She didn't question it. "Okay," she said. "If you need a place to stay, you can come here. I'm in a flat."

That was all I needed. I wasn't ready to stay in an unknown hotel, in an unfamiliar place. I wanted to be with family, to feel the warmth of someone who knew me, even if I was on this journey alone. I had always hidden behind my own walls, but now I was ready to step out and face the world, even if it meant facing it alone.

I took a rickshaw to her place. It was late, and the city was quiet, almost too quiet. The high had worn off, and I was left with only the calm clarity of knowing that this trip was a turning point for me. I wasn't just traveling. I was breaking free.

As I made my way to my sister's flat, the weight of the past year started to sink in. I had come so far. I had spent five years in a cage of my own making, and now, after one year of college, I was finally flying. The journey, the solo trip, everything—it was all part of the process. I was no longer the person who had spent his life hiding in the shadows. I was the person who had broken free, who had spread his wings.

And as I sat in that rickshaw, with the quiet city of Dehradun surrounding me, I realized that the bird had finally taken flight. The cage was broken. And now, the sky was mine.

THE CAGE AND THE FLIGHT

The moment I reached my sister's flat, I felt an unfamiliar sense of peace, a quietness that I hadn't experienced in a while. She greeted me warmly, surprised at how much I had grown since we last saw each other—four years ago. At the time, she was married, living in Dehradun, and her husband was working in Dubai. The distance between us had made it hard to stay close, but today, sitting with her, it felt like home.

We caught up over a cup of tea. She told me I was all grown up now, and I couldn't help but smile at how much I had changed in just a year. It was odd, though, feeling this sense of "growing up" and yet, feeling like I was still so lost in my thoughts. She made me food, and after eating, I retired to her guest room, the quiet of the night wrapping around me as I fell into a deep sleep.

The next morning, she asked me what I wanted for breakfast, and I told her, "Whatever you like." I couldn't shake the sense of confusion that lingered from the night before. I knew I needed to share something with her, something that had been weighing on my chest.

I finally confessed that I had come alone to Dehradun, and she didn't react the way I expected. No surprise, no shock. It was like it didn't faze her. She simply said, "You've grown up, living in Delhi all alone. Coming here alone isn't a big deal for you."

That simple statement made me feel both relieved and conflicted. It was like she saw me in a way no one else did.

As we spoke, she began to reminisce about my childhood. She laughed, recalling how I used to break everything I got my hands on. Radios, toys, even my sister's speakers—I'd take them apart just to see how they worked. I was a curious little troublemaker. She reminded me that I used to call myself "Mastery," a slang I invented, pretending I was some kind of engineer, always tinkering with things. It was funny to hear her talk about it because, in that moment, it hit me—those were my dreams back then. My family used to joke, "He's going to be an engineer someday." I could almost hear their voices echoing in my head.

But something changed. The family that once surrounded me with warmth and noise had all but disappeared. As I grew older, the people I loved moved away for work, for education, for better opportunities. Our once bustling home, filled with laughter and stories, became quieter. The house that once felt alive now felt empty.

My uncle, who had been a pillar in our family, became an officer after clearing the BPSC exams. My other uncle moved to the city, buying a house close to where he worked. My aunt left to find a better future for her children, and soon, I was left in a house with just my parents, my younger brother, and my grandfather. We were five, down from twenty-five.

It was this sudden shift that made me feel the loneliness. The disappearance of those voices, those people I had once shared everything with, left me with a void I couldn't fill. And when my grandmother passed away, the last connection to my childhood world was gone.

I started thinking about what I wanted from life. Education, opportunities, a way out. I had always been a good student, waking up at 4 AM to study as a seven-year-old, a child driven by a desire to prove something—to myself and to everyone around me. I remember the pride in my parents' eyes when they saw my academic achievements. The compliments from teachers, telling my father how talented I was. Those words fueled me, made me believe I could do anything.

That confidence led me to make a big decision: I dropped out of school after sixth grade. At just thirteen, I decided to study on my own, with a private tutor who had been teaching all the children in our family. No one objected. I was a bright child, and everyone trusted that I knew what I was doing.

But the truth was, my childhood dreams, my innocence, started slipping away as I isolated myself from the world. The more I stayed in my little bubble, the more disconnected I became from everyone else. And now, sitting with my sister, I couldn't help but reflect on all that. All the things I had done, all the decisions I had made, and how they had brought me to this point.

And then, just as I was lost in thought, my sister hit me with a question that jolted me out of my reverie: "Do you drink or smoke weed?"

The question caught me off guard. I had always been honest with myself, but hearing it from her felt different. I could see the concern in her eyes, and for a split second,

I felt guilty. She looked at me with that older-sister gaze, disappointed but hopeful. "You've grown up so well, and everyone has faith in you. Why would you do this?"

I couldn't defend myself at that moment. I couldn't tell her that I wasn't hurting anyone. I just nodded, feeling small. "I do it occasionally," I said, not knowing how to explain it any other way.

Her response was simple, "Drinking is fine, occasionally, but not weed." She still believed in me, even though I felt like I was disappointing her. It was a strange mix of guilt and defiance.

After our conversation, I tried to push it all aside. We had lunch, and then she suggested we take a tour of Dehradun. I agreed, though part of me was still reeling from the conversation.

Her friends came over, and we chatted. Her friends seemed impressed by the fact that I was studying at IIT. My sister introduced me, saying, "He's studying in IIT," and I could see the pride in her eyes. They all nodded, saying, "Wow, he must be really intelligent." It felt good, but at the same time, it felt hollow. They didn't know the whole story. They didn't know the loneliness I carried, the conflicts I faced, the isolation I had felt for so many years.

As we headed out to explore Dehradun, I started feeling out of place. My sister's friends kept staring at me, and I could tell they were talking about me. They were nice, but I felt like I was on display, like they were judging me. For the first time, I wished I hadn't opened up to my sister.

Eventually, we reached FRI (Forest Research Institute) in Dehradun. It was an impressive place, established in 1906, with its large open spaces and old architecture. But I couldn't enjoy it. My sister's friends kept asking me to take pictures, and every time I tried to look at the scenery, I felt uncomfortable.

Later, we went to Mussoorie, and that's when things started shifting inside me. We climbed the mountain to George Everest Peak. The more I climbed, the more alive I felt. At first, I moved slowly, but as I pushed myself higher, something inside me clicked. I felt like I was breaking free, like I was finally starting to soar after years of being caged in.

My sister couldn't keep up. Her knees hurt, so I continued on alone. I reached the peak after running for what felt like hours, and when I got there, I felt powerful. There were people smoking, and for a moment, I wanted to join them. But then I saw the faces around me, people who didn't know my past, my struggles. I introduced myself as a student from IIT, and they welcomed me. One of them handed me a cigarette, and for a moment, I felt like I had won—like I had broken free.

The high didn't last long, though. As I headed back down, I couldn't shake the feeling that something had shifted. I had come on this trip to find myself, but all I was doing was running away from the loneliness I had never confronted.

That night, as I packed my things to leave, I realized that I wasn't the person I had hoped to find. I wasn't the carefree traveler I had imagined myself to be. I was still the same person, the same person who had felt trapped in a cage for so long.

I asked my cab driver to take me to the bus stand. When I arrived, I found out that the last buses had already left. The cab driver was gone, and I was stuck in a city that wasn't mine. I had nowhere to go. For the next seven hours, I sat alone at the bus stand, waiting for the first bus back to Delhi.

It was the first time in a long time that I felt completely alone. But even in that solitude, I realized something—I was starting to break free. The cage that had held me for years, the loneliness, the fear, was slowly starting to crumble. I wasn't flying yet, but I was learning how to spread my wings.

The bus came at 4 AM, and I finally made my way back to college. The journey wasn't over, but I knew that the cage I had lived in was no longer my prison. Maybe, just maybe, I was finally ready to fly.

CHAPTER NINETEEN

A CAGE OF UNANSWERED QUESTIONS

After the trip, I returned to the hostel, and as expected, everyone was buzzing with excitement. "Wow, bro, you went for a solo trip to Mussoorie!" they exclaimed. I just shrugged it off. How could I explain that it wasn't entirely solo? That I'd been with my sister for part of it? I didn't know how to break down the complexity of what had happened in my mind. It wasn't just a trip; it was me breaking free from the cage I had been in for so long.

But as the days passed, everything returned to normal. The excitement faded, and reality sank in. It was the end of Semester 3—time had flown by so fast. And just like every other semester before, I hadn't really studied much. But this time, there was something different. Sure, I hadn't read for the exams, but I had learned other things. Things I hadn't planned on learning: how to roll a joint, how to crush weed, how to make a peg, and, most importantly, how to roast people and talk to them in a way that felt natural.

I had learned how to make friends—something I had never really known how to do before.

But amidst all this newfound knowledge and change, one thing kept haunting me. Her. Syra.

It had been a year now, and I still couldn't forget her. I remembered the day I called her, the day I finally worked up the courage to tell her how I felt. My friends—PDS, Shaan, Jitu, and Samarth—had pushed me to do it. They were all tired of hearing me talk about her. They said, "Just call her. Get it over with, man." So I did.

But it didn't go the way I had hoped. I was high, fumbling with my words, not confident enough to express myself properly. It wasn't the version of me I wanted to show her. When I told her how I felt, she just said, "Okay, we'll talk tomorrow," and the call ended.

I felt rejected, but a strange sense of relief washed over me. For months, I had carried this burden of unspoken feelings, and now it was out there. But still, a part of me felt guilty. I hadn't told her in the right way, not like a gentleman. I had been impulsive and messy.

My friends, though, were supportive. "You did it, man! You told her!" they cheered, trying to pump me up. But it didn't feel like a victory.

Months passed, and I heard that Syra had a boyfriend now. I didn't know how to feel. Was I supposed to be upset? Should I still care? But deep down, I knew I couldn't forget her. And with every passing day, it became harder to move on.

At first, I didn't know how to talk to girls. The thought of talking to someone I liked made my heart race like a machine gun. But I had made progress. I had learned how to be more comfortable around people, to hold conversations without being self-conscious. I started focusing on myself—my looks, my style, my voice. I was trying to become someone who could talk to a girl without feeling like I was betraying Syra in the process.

I started growing my hair, trimming my beard, speaking in a deeper voice, and acting more confident. Slowly, my friends noticed the changes. They told me I looked different, like I had grown into myself. And I had.

I wasn't just learning to talk to girls. I was learning to be comfortable in my own skin.

I began to approach girls at the library side and in the lab. I would talk to them casually, just to practice, just to see what it felt like. Every time I spoke to a girl, my heart would beat like a drum. But over time, it got easier. I even downloaded Bumble, trying to test myself, to see if I could get someone's attention. I got good responses, but it was time-consuming, so I eventually deleted it.

But even then, I couldn't shake the feeling that something was missing. I'd see a girl who was attractive, and I'd approach her, but something inside me would scream: *Why isn't this Syra?*

I remember once, I was talking to a girl, and she asked me to hold her hand because she was scared. I did. And in that moment, I felt the strangest sense of emptiness. *Why isn't this Syra's hand?*

I couldn't help it. I tried, but every time I spoke to someone else, I couldn't stop comparing them to her. Nothing felt right. I felt like I was betraying her, even though I knew I had no claim to her anymore.

It was frustrating. Exhausting. After all my effort, I was still stuck on her.

I began to withdraw from the world again. I stopped going to the library at night. I didn't want to face the awkwardness of talking to girls, pretending like I had moved on when, deep down, I hadn't. I felt like I was back to square one. So, I retreated to what was familiar. Weed. I spent my nights in the hostel, smoking and drifting in and out of thoughts, unable to escape the cage of my own mind.

I had changed a lot. I had tried to move on, tried to learn to be someone else, but in the end, I realized something: I hadn't really changed at all. Because no matter what I did, I couldn't forget her.

I didn't know how to let go.

CHANGING FACES, CHANGING WORLDS

The semester break after Semester 3 was a blur. I had barely realized how fast time had passed. I gave all my exams the night before and somehow, *magically*, managed to pass them all. Then came the long holiday in December, one whole month at home that I didn't even feel like I'd spent. Before I knew it, it was January 1, 2024, and I was back at IIT for Semester 4, with a brand new resolution: go to class daily, study every day, and get my act together. I lasted two weeks. For two weeks, I kept my word—showing up to class, trying to keep up with the lectures, and even cracking open the textbooks.

But after those two weeks, I was back to my old ways. I wasn't going to class as regularly anymore, and I wasn't really putting in the effort to study. But something had changed in me. I wasn't the same person I had been a few months ago. Now, I was comfortable with everyone. I wasn't nervous about talking to people, whether it was the seniors, my classmates, or strangers. I was *one of them*. No one would look at me and think, "That guy used to be an introvert."

I had completely changed, and I gave all the credit to one thing—weed. Weed had been the catalyst for my transformation. It was the reason I was now able to interact with people, take life less seriously, and *be* someone else—someone who wasn't afraid to live a little. Anmol, who was once just a distant friend, had now become one of my closest. Samarth and I, however, seemed to have drifted apart. There was something that had shifted between us, a gap that had started to form. Maybe it was because I had changed so much and Samarth hadn't, or maybe it was something else, but I started feeling like we were no longer on the same wavelength. I didn't pay too much attention to it though, because I had other friends to keep me busy.

One of those new friends was Om. Om became my closest companion. He was like a reflection of the old me, but more mature, more emotionally stable, and, surprisingly, practical. I remember teaching him how to smoke a cigarette just the way Harish Sir had taught me. Later, I taught him and some of his friends— Hritik, and Ayush Niranjan—how to smoke weed. Cigarettes and weed became the reason we bonded so closely. We spent a lot of time together, and in those moments, I felt like I could finally connect with people on a deeper level.

But as time passed, I realized something—this semester was quickly slipping away. I wasn't focusing on academics at all. Instead, I found myself getting more and more involved in a different kind of distraction—poker.

It all started when a guy from my department, Utsav Gupta, brought a poker set to our hostel. I had never played before, but Utsav and the others taught us. At first, I was terrible. The first day I played, I lost all my chips. But I didn't mind. The game itself was fun, and the more I played, the more I got better at it. Eventually, I started playing regularly with a new group of people: Shaan, Shayan, Anmol, Abheek, Karthik, and Yagya. These were the *real* IITians—the guys who excelled in academics, went to class every day, never touched weed or any other form of intoxication, and spoke like gentlemen.

They had no idea what kind of impact I was going to have on their lives.

We started playing poker more and more, and soon it became a daily thing. There were two wings in our hostel: one where we smoked weed and played poker, and another wing—what we called the "Electrical Wing"—where poker was played without any intoxication. The more I played, the better I got. I started winning more, taking bigger pots. People started to believe I was cheating because I won so much, but the truth was simple: it was all mathematics. I had learned to calculate the probabilities in my head, and with some intuition, I was almost always right.

By now, I had become *the guy* to beat at poker. If I was in the game, people knew they had little chance of winning. It wasn't luck; it was pure skill. Eventually, I started visiting other hostels to play poker. And the results were always the same—I won. I won a lot of money, but I never kept it. I gave it all back to the guys because, for me, it wasn't about the money—it was about the thrill of the game, the confidence it gave me, and the sense of control it offered.

So now, my life was revolving around two things: weed and poker. It wasn't the healthiest combination, but I was having fun. I was getting closer to the people in Shaan, Shayan, and Karthik's wing. I began spending a lot of time with Karthik because we shared something in common—both of us were from the same hometown. That connection drew us together, and soon we were talking daily. Karthik was one of the few people I met who was grounded, kind, and always ready with good advice. He was a great debater and someone who had his life figured out much more than I did.

Alongside Karthik, I also began interacting more with Vijay and Abhimanyu Tiwari—two roommates in the Electrical Wing. They were smart, well-spoken, and definitely in control of their lives. But there was this one incident with Vijay that stands out in my mind.

One evening, Vijay called us in a panic. He'd gotten into some trouble at another hostel and some guys were threatening to beat him up. Samarth came to me and said, "Someone's threatening to beat Vijay. Let's go help him." I was high at the time, but something in me clicked. I grabbed a broken hockey stick I found lying around, threw on my jacket, and rushed out. The whole hostel was buzzing—everyone was following me as I marched toward the other hostel.

When we arrived, the guard looked at me, holding the hockey stick, and I casually said, "How's it going?" He replied, "Good," and didn't seem to care at all. I kept walking, heading straight for Vijay's room. When I got there, I found him sitting and eating pizza. It turned out the whole situation was completely blown out of proportion. There was no threat. He was fine.

But the whole experience was a turning point for me. I had become someone who acted without thinking, who was willing to step up for my friends—even when the situation was far from serious. It was a weird kind of bravery, and it was a side of me that had emerged from the combination of the people I surrounded myself with, the lifestyle I was leading, and the choices I was making.

I had fully embraced this new version of myself, but somewhere deep down, I was still wondering—was this who I wanted to be?

CHAPTER TWENTY-ONE

THE SHIFT IN THE WIND

After meeting the people from the Electrical Wing, I couldn't stop thinking about how disciplined and balanced their lives were. These guys knew how to enjoy life, but they also studied hard and worked together. The contrast between them and my old group was striking. On one hand, there were the guys in my old wing—smoking weed, playing poker, watching web series, and losing themselves in FIFA games. On the other hand, the Electrical Wing guys were focused on assignments, hitting the books, sleeping at regular hours, and preparing for a bright future.

I couldn't help but admire the way they carried themselves—intellectual, driven, and focused. There was something about their lifestyle that attracted me. Slowly, I began to realize that this was the kind of life I wanted for myself. I had been stuck in a pattern of self-destruction, living for the next high, the next poker game, the next party. But now, I was tired of it. I was exhausted—waking up at odd hours, sleeping through the afternoons, running on fumes. I wanted a change.

I made up my mind. I was going to switch wings. I walked up to Vijay and said, "I want to come to your room."

He and Abhimanyu were the only two in the room, and Vijay was happy to accommodate me. But there was one condition: "I don't smoke in the room." That was easy for me, actually—it aligned with my desire to leave the old habits behind.

So, I packed my things and moved into the Electrical Wing. My old wingmates weren't happy about it. They started questioning me: "Why are you doing this? You've changed, man!" Anmol didn't say anything, but Om wasn't thrilled. He just said, "It's your decision."

When Samarth came to visit my new room, he asked, "Let's go to our old room." I told him, "No, I'll stay here. I'm just here for a month." But I was lying to him—and to myself. This wasn't a temporary thing. I was done with my old wing. Shantanu, too, wasn't happy. Malik said something like, "You don't understand, do you?"

All these words, all the pushback, made me feel like I had won. I was no longer the introverted kid who was scared to talk to anyone. I wasn't the person I used to be. I was something different now, something more. And the change had a ripple effect. Our old hangout spot, ED32, started losing its vibe. No one was sitting there anymore. But people from my old wing started coming to my new room, EC28. Slowly, EC28 became the new hangout spot. Poker sessions began happening there instead of ED32. The old wing, which had felt so alive, now seemed to have a new energy. EC28 was alive with people laughing, talking, and playing poker. Even the Electrical Wing, which had seemed like a group of robotic, disciplined people, began to change. They started joining in, picking up poker, loosening up.

And as I spent more time with them, I began to change, too. I started doing things I hadn't done before—things that felt productive, meaningful. I started coding. It was something I'd never really paid attention to before, but the guys in my new wing were all into it, and their work ethic rubbed off on me. I had always been good at math, and I knew that coding was a skill that could take me places. Slowly, I started spending hours every day learning coding, building projects, solving problems.

The old me would never have considered it. But now, I was becoming a different version of myself. And it felt good. I had gone from being someone who would waste whole days away smoking and playing poker to someone who was learning a new skill. In just one month, I went from knowing almost nothing about coding to becoming good at it.

This transformation wasn't just happening in the way I worked. It was happening in the way I thought, in the way I carried myself. I began acting more intellectual, more like the people I had surrounded myself with. But I couldn't completely escape my old habits. Weed and cigarettes were still part of my life, and they weren't going anywhere anytime soon. Slowly, I noticed that some of the guys I spent time with—guys I respected for their discipline and focus—started picking up some of my habits. Karthik, for instance, started smoking cigarettes with me, and Abhimanyu, who had smoked before, began smoking more regularly.

It was like a weird exchange—these guys were giving me new habits, good ones, like focusing on coding and becoming more disciplined. And in return, I was passing on my habits to them—like smoking cigarettes.

Soon, our little group of smokers expanded. Abheek, who had smoked occasionally before, became a regular smoker after seeing me and Abhimanyu. Even Shaan, who had always kept to himself, started smoking with us. It felt like the old me was back in a way, but with a twist—this time, I was doing it with the people I respected most.

At times, things got crazier. I remember one night when Abhinmanyu, Abheek, and I were hanging out in my new room. I asked, "Wanna do a bong?" Abhinav said, "Why not?" Abheek was game, too. So I went to my old room, grabbed the weed pouch, and came back to EC28 with the bong. We crushed the weed and started smoking.

The balcony of my new wing was a perfect place for smoking—it was high up, with a view of a bridge and a lot of trees. No one could see us, and it gave us the sense of freedom we craved. After finishing the bong, we suddenly had a craving for ice cream. So, we went to Holistic, a night mess near the campus that opened only at night. We grabbed some ice cream, and as we were eating, Abheek said, "Let's go to the haunted bridge."

Now, the "haunted bridge" wasn't really haunted. It was just a secluded part of campus that no one really visited. But for us, it was the perfect place to go when we were high. We walked toward the bridge, laughing, feeling the rush of doing something a little bit wild. As we neared the bridge, we heard a dog barking. But we didn't think much of it.

That's when we reached the bridge—a wooden structure that spanned a drainage canal. We climbed up, laughing, feeling like we were on some sort of adventure. But as we crossed to the other side, we noticed something strange. A dog, barking from behind a netted boundary. We didn't see it clearly, but it felt like we were in danger.

Without thinking, the three of us started running as fast as we could, down an unfamiliar path. The adrenaline was pumping, and we were laughing and gasping for breath. We didn't stop until we reached the other side of campus, and when we finally looked back, we saw something that made us freeze.

A figure—a man—was walking toward us, holding something that looked like an axe. His face was partially hidden, but it looked like he was heading straight for us. We didn't know what to think. We thought it was some kind of serial killer. Without another second's hesitation, we took off running faster than before. We didn't stop until we reached the safety of the hostel.

It was one of those nights that felt surreal—half fear, half thrill, all adrenaline. And somehow, it felt like the perfect snapshot of where my life was at that point: uncertain, wild, and unpredictable. But, strangely, it felt right. Like I was exactly where I needed to be.

FINDING MY FOOTING

I slowly started winning in life. One day, I remember there was a competitive programming contest. It happens online every week, and I had started participating in these contests regularly with my friends. As the weeks went by, I kept improving. One day, I solved 3 out of the 5 questions in the contest. Even Vijay and Abhimanyu couldn't do that, and Karthik only solved three as well. It felt like a small victory, but a victory nonetheless.

After the contest, we all went to Sassi, a small place near our hostel, where smokers would gather. I had already mentioned it before. It became a habit to go there almost every day, sometimes even two or three times a day. That day, after the contest, me, Abhimanyu, and Karthik walked over to Sassi, and out of nowhere, I saw Om.

He already knew I had solved three questions in the contest, and he was genuinely happy to see me doing something productive with my time. It felt good to hear him say that. It was the kind of validation I needed at that moment. It gave me confidence that after a year and a half of wasting time, I was finally doing something for my future. But the truth is, I didn't feel guilty or angry at myself. I understood myself better now. I knew that a year-long gap wasn't the end of the world. I had been exhausted, both physically and mentally, but I was getting back into the race.

I had missed out on a lot, watching people move forward in life while I stayed stuck. But now, I was catching up. Slowly but surely, I was gaining confidence and skills, especially in coding. But I knew that wasn't enough. These small wins in coding weren't going to make me successful overnight. I always wanted instant success, like winning the lottery. I dreamt of changing my life in a single moment—financial independence, freedom.

Money had always been the barrier to that freedom. If I had enough of it, I could do whatever I wanted. I could live life on my own terms. The more I thought about it, the more I realized that my childhood dreams—those sci-fi movies, the idea of building something as revolutionary as Iron Man's suit or creating space technology—were just that: dreams. The reality hit harder. What had happened to that ambition?

Where did it all go wrong? I asked myself. The main reason was the isolation. My period of isolation from the real world had made me forget my dreams and lose touch with reality. Sometimes, I'd wonder if I had the same brain as Shaan, the sharp, intellectual mind. If I did, why was I wasting time with assignments? Why was I stuck doing meaningless tasks? I had always challenged the traditional rules of life. I didn't want to be part of the rat race. I had already "won" that race in my childhood, and that realization had set me free.

I didn't want to be a servant to anyone. I wanted to lead a revolution of my own. But during my time alone, I had learned a few things about myself. I developed a habit of writing motivational quotes and life lessons. I had a small diary that I carried with me, but when I first came to IIT, I had stopped writing in it. The isolation had pushed me into a place where I didn't think about my goals anymore.

But that day, as I sat there, I decided to open that diary. I started reading what I had written in the past, and I couldn't help but laugh at myself. What the hell was I thinking back then? My childish dreams seemed almost laughable now. But then, I realized something important: maybe being childish is the key to staying focused and making consistent efforts toward your goals.

In my diary, I had written down clear goals. I had aimed to top the BSEB 10th exam and earn a scholarship to go to Kota for IIT coaching. But I didn't achieve that. I didn't even top the district. However, I did top my school, which had around 500 students. Even though I didn't achieve the exact goals I had set, I still made progress. And yet, I didn't have the courage to tell my father that I wanted to go to Kota. So, I let go of that dream, and instead, I used the government scholarship to buy a brand-new phone.

The second plan, the dream of escaping from home after topping in the BSEB class 12th exam and going to Kota, also failed. I didn't top the state, but I did top my district, which still felt like an achievement. Once again, though, my plan of leaving home and living independently didn't materialize the way I had hoped.

So, I created a new plan. I would study for IIT JEE, not for anyone else, but for myself. I'd work hard, and eventually, I would get into any IIT college. Six months of hard work later, I did get into IIT, and at that moment, escaping from home seemed like a victory. It wasn't easy, but it was my dream finally coming true after so many years of effort. The sense of independence I longed for was becoming a reality.

But one thing lingered in my mind: I never told my father that I wanted to leave home and live on my own. I had always wanted to be completely free, financially independent, and self-sufficient. So, I devised plans where I wouldn't need money from my family, and somehow, I believed that if I made it to IIT, I'd figure it all out on my own.

But now, more than a year and a half into my journey, my college fees are still being covered by my father, and that reality hits harder than I expected. It hurts deeply. This is not how I imagined things would go. I thought I'd be independent by now. The realization stings—the freedom I sought, the success I wanted, is still out of reach. It feels like I'm failing in life, despite all the progress I've made.

CHAPTER TWENTY-THREE

A NEW BEGINNING

I decided to pursue my writing habit more seriously. I started writing down my daily thoughts, life lessons, and reflections on my laptop. I burned some of the pages from my old diary. It felt symbolic, as if I was leaving my old self behind. It was a fresh start, and for the first time in a long while, I felt like I was truly moving forward.

My life started to take a positive turn. No more crying before bed, no more loneliness. Slowly, I became the reason for others to smile. Karthik always seemed happy whenever he saw me, and Om and Hritik did too. Vijay, with his usual positive energy, would greet me with a grin every time we crossed paths. I could feel the shift within myself. I was becoming the person who could lift others, make them feel better, and be a source of positivity.

One day, something unexpected happened. I received a message on Instagram from a girl at my college. It wasn't anything special at first. She had replied to one of my Instagram notes, which were usually filled with humor or funny stories. I had this habit of updating my Instagram stories occasionally, just sharing where I was, what I was doing, or what I was vibing with at that moment. It wasn't regular, but whenever I felt like sharing, I would. And she replied to one of those.

We exchanged a few messages, but I didn't pay too much attention to it. I wasn't really looking for any female interaction at that time. I was happy with my life and focused on my growth. But then, a few days later, she messaged me again. This time, it felt different. Maybe it was a sign, a message from the universe telling me that my life was getting back on track.

She was the topper of IIT-JEE, one of the brightest in the college. But honestly, I didn't care much about people's achievements. I treated everyone the same, whether it was the college guard or the professors. I respected everyone equally. But for some reason, I felt drawn to her. There was something about her intellect, her way of thinking, that caught my attention. So, I asked her where she was. She replied, saying she was in the library, as expected.

We started talking more, and eventually, we decided to meet. I went to the library, and we talked for hours—about 3-4 hours, in fact. I had never had such a long conversation with any girl on campus, let alone walking near the library. She spoke about how she felt disconnected from the people around her. They were all obsessed with marks, always trying to bring her down when she did poorly. She talked about how she wanted to break free from that world, escape from the expectations, and experience some adventure in life.

In that moment, I thought to myself, *Wow, she chose the right person at the right time.* I didn't think anyone else on campus would be as adventurous as I was. We connected over our shared sense of wanting something different, something beyond just grades and success. After hours of talking, I walked her to a place just before the girls' hostel. Then, I headed back to the hostel myself.

When I met Karthik later, I couldn't hold back. I told him everything—about her, about the conversations, about how different she was from everyone else. Karthik, being the friend who knew me best, was supportive. He said, "Good, keep it up. Maybe she will help you move away from your bad habits." He mentioned that maybe she could be the one to help me leave behind the intoxication that had been a part of my life for so long.

I heard what Karthik said, but I didn't really listen. Intoxication, to me, was a personal choice. I didn't think a girl could change that. I believed it was something I had to work through myself, not something someone else could fix for me. But what I did feel good about was the fact that she was the first girl after Syra that didn't make me feel like I was comparing her to my past. I felt like I was moving on, and that realization filled me with a sense of relief.

We met a few more times, and I started to share more about myself with her. I told her about my habits, about how I felt about my life, and how I was trying to improve. She told me to leave those bad habits behind, but I didn't really take her words seriously. I just told her, "I'll think about it." I even mentioned that we were completely different—like the diagonals of a square. She disagreed at first, saying that all people were the same, that grades didn't matter. Her perspective on life was refreshing, and I found myself liking her more for the way she saw the world.

She seemed like the kind of person who could live independently, someone who didn't need anyone to validate her existence. I admired that. But at the same time, I began to think, *Maybe I'm not the right guy for her.* Maybe I didn't deserve her friendship. So, I started distancing myself, ignoring her messages. And, in turn, she stopped replying as well.

One day, I made a mistake. I sent her a video of me doing intoxication. I wasn't supposed to send it, but I did. She didn't respond right away, but after that, she stopped talking to me altogether. It wasn't a dramatic breakup or anything, but we both silently let it go. My last message was seen, but it wasn't replied to. But honestly, I wasn't upset.

In fact, I felt like a weight had been lifted off me. After 1.5 years, I had finally freed myself from Syra's shadow. I wasn't emotionally attached anymore. I had moved on. Or at least, I thought I had.

I couldn't help but wonder, *Am I really free from her, or is this just a fleeting feeling?*

CHAPTER TWENTY-FOUR

THE BURDEN OF INFLUENCE

I had spent so much time blaming my circumstances, blaming the people around me, for everything that had gone wrong in my life. But one day, I realized something that shook me to the core. It wasn't them—my friends, my peers, my environment—that was holding me back. It was me. I wasn't the one being influenced by others; I was the bad influence.

I had been so blind to the damage I was causing. With my old group, I thought I was simply wasting time. But the truth was, they were wasting their time with me. I dragged them into my world of distractions, chaos, and self-doubt. And then, I saw the same thing happening in the electrical wing, the place I thought I could escape to. I thought I was doing better, but instead, I was repeating the same patterns. I had unknowingly started to influence these people, leading them down the same path of poor choices.

Vijay, who was known for being one of the most sober guys in our group, also started to follow my lead. It began innocently enough. He started vaping, something I had started doing just to fit in, to escape from the pressure that was slowly suffocating me. But it didn't stop there. Soon, he wanted more. He asked me for alcohol. I remember giving him that bottle full of *LIT* during the House Day celebrations at the hostel—something I had brought for myself, something I had used as a crutch. At that moment, I realized just how much the dynamics in our wing had changed since my arrival. I was no longer the one being influenced. I had become the one influencing others. And it wasn't a positive influence.

That realization hit me harder than I expected. I wasn't the one who needed saving. I was the one who needed to save others, but I was too lost in my own mess to even see it. I had dragged people into my darkness, and now I had to face the consequences of my actions.

In the midst of this heavy reflection, I went back to my old room, hoping that being in a familiar place would bring me some comfort. But the truth hit me like a brick: **I couldn't run from my own reality**. I had made my bed, and now I had to lie in it. I had spent so much time trying to escape, to avoid the consequences of my actions, but the truth was inescapable.

The Mid-Semester Struggle

It was about ten days before the end-semester exams when I realized that I had no energy left to keep running. I had worked harder for my midterms this time. In the past, I had waited until the night before to study, always managing to scrape by. But this time, I started preparing a week in advance. I thought I was doing things differently. I was trying to change.

But despite my efforts, I couldn't meet my own expectations. I had studied harder than ever, yet the results weren't as satisfying as I had hoped. I scored a little better than usual, but it wasn't enough. It was never enough. I felt a growing sense of disappointment in myself. The pressure was crushing, and I couldn't handle it anymore. I thought I was making progress, but I wasn't. I couldn't escape this feeling of inadequacy. I wasn't just failing at my exams; I was failing at life.

By the time the end-semester exams rolled around, I had nothing left. No fuel. No motivation. I had poured all my energy into trying to fix myself, but I hadn't fixed anything at all. I had nothing left to give. I was numb.

The Escape Home

With the exams over, I just wanted to leave. I couldn't stay at the campus any longer. The pressure, the confusion, the emptiness—it was all too much. I wanted to go home, to be with my family, to be far away from the college, from the weight of my failures. But the electrical wing had plans to go on a trip to McLeodganj. They were excited, making plans, joking around. They seemed so carefree, so full of energy. And I couldn't bear it. I couldn't face their excitement when I felt so lost.

I had already booked my ticket home. I couldn't cancel it. I needed to leave. And so, three days after the exams, I packed my things and left, hoping that maybe, just maybe, being away from this place would bring me the clarity I so desperately needed.

But when I got home, the quiet didn't bring the relief I had hoped for. It only gave me more time to reflect on my failures, my choices. One week later, as I was trying to get back to a sense of normalcy, I received an email from the IIT. **Summer semester was starting in three days.** I had to return to campus to complete a course I had withdrawn from in my second semester. If I didn't, I would face a degree extension.

I couldn't face my father with this truth. I couldn't tell him that I had failed. I couldn't admit that I was struggling. So, for the first time in my life, I lied to him. I told him that I had to return to college to work on my project under a professor, and that my internship would follow after that. He believed me. He said, "Do what you need to do," and I was left with the weight of my own lie.

The Return to Campus

When I returned to the campus, the atmosphere was completely different. The hostel was almost empty. There were only a few familiar faces—Karthik, Maanav, and Saif. I had spent the entire semester avoiding them, trying to figure out what went wrong with me. But now, as I walked into the hostel, I was faced with the reality of my isolation.

Maanav, who had always been the quiet one, lived his life in his own mysterious way. He didn't care much about academics, and he never went home. He lived in the hostel year-round, always moving from one semester to the next, without any real break. He had always been there, but I never truly understood him until now. He never shared his feelings with anyone. He only spoke when it was necessary, when someone roamed into his territory. But I knew there was more to him than what met the eye.

Saif, Karthik, and Abheek—roommates—were disciplined and focused, but there was something about them that made me feel small. Saif, in particular, seemed to see right through me. I remember a conversation we had a long time ago. He reminded me of the first day in the hostel when everyone gathered in one room, asking me what I was doing there. I had replied, "I'm here to have fun." They all laughed, and that was the moment I became part of their circle. But now, it felt different. Saif looked at me differently now, with respect, almost as if he could see the change in me, the transformation that had happened, for better or worse.

The Moment of Pain

One night, I walked into the campus with a sense of dread hanging over me. The loneliness felt more intense than ever. And then, in the midst of that silence, I saw her. **Syra.** I didn't expect it. I didn't want to see her. But there she was, standing with someone else—her boyfriend.

The world around me blurred. All the emotions I thought I had buried rushed back in an instant. For months, I had convinced myself that I had moved on, that I was fine. But seeing her with him shattered that illusion. My heart broke in a way I didn't know was possible. It was as if I had been holding my breath for so long, and now I was drowning in the weight of my own emotions.

I couldn't take it anymore. I left the scene, my heart heavy with pain. I went to the SDA near the main gate of the college, a place where students often gathered to smoke and escape. I bought a pack of cigarettes, a bottle of Coke, and I called Maanav. I told him, "Let's drink. I need to forget tonight."

I went back to the hostel, grabbed two glasses, and took a bottle of Old Monk that Karthik had brought back for me from McLeodganj. He wasn't around—he had gone to visit his aunt in Delhi. I opened the bottle, poured the liquor, and invited Maanav to drink with me.

We sat there, drunk, talking in broken words, both of us hiding behind the alcohol. I told Maanav about Syra. I told him how I thought I had moved on, but I hadn't. The pain was still there, lingering in the background. And then, unexpectedly, Maanav opened up about a pain I hadn't known about. A girl he had loved, a girl who had died in an accident before he could confess his feelings. He had never told anyone, not even me.

In that moment, as the alcohol clouded our minds, I realized something that hit me harder than anything I had ever felt before: **We all carry our own burdens, but sometimes we never show them.** Maanav had been laughing and joking with me for so long, but I had never known the depth of his pain. And now, I understood.

We spent the rest of the night on the terrace, clinging to each other as if we were the only two people who could understand what the other was going through. It was in that moment that I promised myself something: I would face my pain head-on, alone if necessary, and get through it.

CHAPTER TWENTY-FIVE

THE AWAKENING

The night of that revelatory moment with Maanav on the terrace stayed with me. When we both stumbled back into the hostel, feeling both drunk and emotionally raw, I could hardly recognize myself anymore. I was floating in this strange limbo, unsure of what I was running towards or away from, but certain of one thing: I couldn't keep running from my own emotions.

That night, after everything calmed down, I ended up sleeping on Karthik's bed, simply because I couldn't bear the thought of being alone. He was away visiting his aunt in Delhi, and the hostel was eerily quiet. I woke up around 1 p.m. to the sound of Karthik's cheerful voice calling out from the doorway. "Wake up, cutie," he said, his voice full of warmth. It was such a relief to see him back. For the first time in days, I felt something like comfort.

We went for a bath, a much-needed reset, and then headed to the library to study. The library was quieter than usual. Most of the students there were preparing for internships, but I knew deep down that I would never be part of that race. I wasn't like the others. I could already see the path my life was going to take, and it wasn't going to include internships, at least not in the way everyone else thought about them. I didn't care about working for a company. The very idea made me feel suffocated.

For as long as I could remember, I had always wanted **freedom**. I had grown up dreaming of a life where I could make my own rules, create my own path, not live under the constraints of a nine-to-five job. The thought of working in a corporate environment, following someone else's orders, giving up my independence, terrified me. So, I knew—I wasn't going to chase the internship dream. But if I wasn't going to do that, what was I supposed to do?

And then, the thought hit me like a bolt of lightning: *Why not create my own company?*

I'd never thought about it in such a direct way, but suddenly, the idea felt right. A sense of clarity washed over me, and I felt more energy coursing through me than I had in ages. **This** was the thing I had been searching for all along. This was the direction I was meant to go in. I didn't need a corporate job. I could create something on my own.

The idea consumed me. My mind started racing with possibilities. What kind of company would I start? What would it be like? What problem would I solve? My mind was spinning as I walked back to my room, lost in thought.

The campus was quiet, emptier than usual, which only gave more space for my ideas to grow. Samarth was at home, so I didn't have access to weed, but my craving for distraction pushed me to call him anyway. When he gave me the number for the dealer, I wasn't even sure what I was doing. But I told myself, *Why not?* It was just one more thing to do, a way to keep the mind sharp for my new project.

I remember the nervous energy I felt waiting for the dealer. The man was late, 45 minutes late, and during that time, I began questioning myself. What if the cops came? What if this was a mistake? But when the dealer finally arrived, I couldn't stop myself. I took the weed, went back to my room, crushed it, and mixed it with some tobacco in my bong. The sensation of the smoke filling my lungs was strangely grounding. It was as if I had unlocked another layer of my mind. I took three big hits, then sat down, feeling both calm and clear at the same time.

And then, as if by magic, I began brainstorming.

The first thing that came to mind was Anmol. He had spent almost two years in IIT without a girlfriend, and it was obvious how badly he wanted one. I looked around the hostel—seventy-five students in total—and realized only three of them had girlfriends. The disparity was shocking. Almost every guy wanted a girlfriend but couldn't get one. Why? I began running scenarios in my mind. Was it the ratio of men to women in IIT? Or was there something deeper at play?

Suddenly, I had the realization: **Why not go outside the IIT to find someone?** But then I thought about the amount of time that would require, and I quickly discarded that idea. No one had the time or patience for that, especially with everything else going on in their lives.

But then, I thought of something else: *People spent hours on Instagram, right? Why not leverage social media for this problem?*

The idea began to take form in my mind. I remembered my own struggles with online dating, specifically with **Bumble**. I had put in so much effort, created a profile, swiped endlessly, but never got a match. I'd seen a video once where a YouTuber made two accounts, one for a girl and one for a boy. The girl's account got 60 matches within a few hours, while the boy's account got nothing. It was a perfect demonstration of the inequality in the dating world, and it struck me.

Why was it that women had so much power in this space? Why wasn't there a platform where both genders had equal opportunity? **Why couldn't both men and women have equal say in who they were connected with?**

That was the moment I realized: **I had found my problem statement.** Now, I just needed a solution. This wasn't just about finding a girlfriend—it was about addressing inequality in the online dating world. I had found something worth solving, and I knew I could do it.

I spent the rest of the night brainstorming solutions. My head was spinning with ideas, and I barely noticed when I drifted into sleep. When I woke up at 4 a.m., I felt a renewed sense of clarity. The high from the weed had faded, but the ideas were still there. I went back to the bong, took a few more hits, and let the ideas pour out of me.

What if I created a platform where people could log in, make accounts, and connect live with others, only when they were ready to date? They wouldn't have to be constantly swiping left or right; they could simply engage when they wanted to. It was a **live dating platform**—a way to meet others without the pressure of traditional online dating apps.

The concept felt revolutionary. The more I thought about it, the more I realized it had legs. I could make this work. I got to work on it immediately, and by the morning, I rushed to Karthik's room, bursting with excitement.

"Karthik, I have an idea. A real one," I said.

He looked at me, half-sleepy but intrigued. "What is it?"

I told him everything. Every detail. The live platform, the concept of equal power between men and women in online dating, the platform where you could connect when ready and disconnect when you weren't.

"Nice," Karthik said after hearing me out. "I like it. You should work on it."

We sat there, bouncing ideas off each other, and then it hit me: *What should we name it?*

"Igloo," I said, almost out of nowhere.

The name just came to me, and Karthik and Saif both liked it instantly. It was simple, unique, and it felt right. But then, as I thought about it more, I realized something even more interesting: **Igloo** was a combination of the two nicknames my parents used for me—my father called me "ILU," and my mother called me "Golu." Combining the two—ILU + **Golu**—became **Igloo**. It felt perfect.

It was the first time in my IIT life that I felt a deep sense of purpose. I had finally found something I was excited about. A real project, a real mission. I started learning web development to build the platform. I watched videos on HTML, CSS, and JavaScript. The more I learned, the more excited I became. I was completely immersed in it. This was no longer just an idea—it was something tangible, something I could build.

Days turned into weeks, and I poured everything I had into Igloo. I would wake up, crush some weed, take a few hits from the bong, and then go to the library to work on the website. I spent every waking hour either coding or brainstorming ideas for Igloo. When I returned to the hostel at night, I did the same thing—weed, bong, and back to work. It became a cycle. But it was a cycle that fueled me, one that made me feel alive in a way I had never felt before.

In the midst of all this, I realized something else: I had been so consumed with regret, with my past, with the things I had missed out on, that I had never taken the time to reflect on my journey, my growth. I had always wanted to write a memoir, to share my story. So, I started doing just that. Every day, I'd sit down and write about my life—the things I'd learned, the mistakes I'd made, the regrets I carried. It felt cathartic. It felt like I was finally taking control of my narrative.

I had two passions now: building Igloo and writing my memoir. And for the first time in my life, I felt like I was finally doing something that mattered.

CHAPTER TWENTY-SIX

REFLECTIONS OF MY JOURNEY

My life had taken a positive turn. I wasn't wasting time anymore. The self-destructive habits of my past seemed to have been replaced by a new sense of purpose. Every minute of my day was either invested in my startup or spent writing my memoir. Writing wasn't a difficult task—it wasn't some grand art form. It was just me, writing down what I felt, what I had lived, and how my experiences shaped who I had become. It wasn't for anyone else. It wasn't to impress. It was just me, explaining myself. Every sentence I wrote, I imagined talking to someone—explaining things to them as I explained them to myself.

I began my memoir from the day I stepped into IIT for the first time. That first day was vivid in my memory—the nervous excitement, the strange mix of independence and uncertainty. As I continued writing, I dug deeper into my memories, reflecting on my journey from a confused teenager to someone who had started to carve his own path. Slowly but surely, the words flowed, and I learned more about myself than I ever expected. In parallel, I was learning everything I could about building my startup—websites, coding, business management, and everything in between. My life had become a blur of learning, creating, and reflecting.

I wasn't the same person I had been when I first entered college. I was more focused, more productive, more aware of my own potential. I had a direction, and I was heading straight for it.

The summer semester ended, and Semester 5 began. The entire campus came alive again with students rushing to their classes, buzzing about their next steps. It was that time of year—the time for internships. Everyone seemed to be preparing with single-minded focus. People were studying for interviews, attending mock sessions, tweaking their resumes, and making sure they were ready for the toughest companies out there.

Karthik and Saif, the two of my closest friends, were preparing relentlessly. I had no doubt in my mind that they would land internships at prestigious companies like Quant or top-tier financial firms. These guys were hardworking and dedicated, always pushing themselves to do their best. I had seen their commitment firsthand—the late nights, the hours spent solving complex problems, and their unwavering pursuit of excellence. I was certain they would both make it big.

But when the first day of internship interviews came, something unexpected happened. None of them got an offer. Not Karthik. Not Saif. Not even Samarth, who I had always believed had the potential to succeed in anything he set his mind to.

It was an eye-opener for me. Here were three of the smartest, most hardworking people I knew, and yet, they didn't get a single internship offer. I couldn't make sense of it. After all the effort they had put in, the late nights, the preparation, how could they not have landed something?

As the days passed, the rejections kept piling up. Day after day, I watched as my friends struggled with the same outcome. No internship. No offer. And I was left questioning everything I had believed about success, hard work, and the path that everyone was so desperately trying to follow.

I found myself thinking about what companies really wanted from students. What were they looking for when they decided whether someone was worthy of an internship? What qualities were they assessing in their candidates? I began to question the very structure of the system we were all operating in.

As I thought more about this, I realized something. If Karthik, Saif, or Samarth had been in my company, I wouldn't have to worry about anything. They all had that sharp, analytical mind, that drive. But then I stopped myself. I realized that it wasn't just about talent. It wasn't just about being smart. It was about vision. And I wondered: did they have the vision?

These were incredibly talented people, yes. But had they ever done anything beyond simply following the well-worn path? Were they so focused on doing well in exams and assignments that they had never taken the time to think about the bigger picture? To think about what they wanted from life beyond just securing a high-paying job at a big company?

I began to realize that my friends, despite their brilliance, were caught up in a race. A race that didn't lead anywhere meaningful. They were competing for jobs, for internships, for salaries, but they had no vision for what they truly wanted to achieve in life. They were working hard, yes—but they were working hard to fit into a system that didn't value creativity or individuality. And that system wasn't the path I wanted to follow.

The more I thought about it, the more I began to see the gap between us. While they were focused on securing the next step in the corporate ladder, I was focused on something else entirely: freedom. The freedom to build something of my own, something that didn't require following the same old rules.

On the other hand, I saw some of my friends succeeding in the traditional system. Shaan and Shayan, for example, had secured impressive internships at a Quant company, earning a 5-lakh-per-month salary. I was genuinely happy for them. They were winning in the system that everyone else was competing in. They had made it to the top, at least for now.

But even as I congratulated them, I couldn't help but ask, "What if a new company came along and offered you more than what you're making now? Would you join that company?"

Without hesitation, they both answered yes. And then Shayan said something that stuck with me: "Why would I leave a company that's paying me well? Why would I work for a startup, especially for something like Igloo?"

That was the moment I realized the truth. What I was building, what I was working on, wasn't something they would consider. It wasn't a step in the path they were on. And maybe that's the way it was supposed to be.

They were following the traditional path—the path that guaranteed success in terms of salary, prestige, and stability. I, on the other hand, was walking a different path. My goal wasn't to secure a high-paying job at a top company. My goal was to create something new, something unique, something that could give me the freedom to build, to innovate, and to live life on my terms.

It wasn't about the money. It wasn't about the job title. It was about creating something that would change the way people thought about relationships, social interaction, and the way we connect with others. Igloo, my startup, was about more than just a product—it was about creating a new kind of space, a new kind of platform that could change lives. It wasn't just about filling the gaps that traditional dating platforms left open; it was about redefining the way people connect.

And in that moment, I realized something crucial: **I wasn't looking for validation from anyone. I wasn't trying to prove myself in a race that wasn't mine.** What I was building wasn't for everyone—and that was okay. Not everyone was ready for what I was trying to create. And that, too, was okay.

While my friends were chasing internships and salaries, I was chasing a vision. A vision of freedom, creativity, and building something that mattered. It was a long road, and it wasn't going to be easy. But I was more convinced than ever that this was the right path for me. The race that my friends were running wasn't the race I was in—and for the first time, I was okay with that.

It wasn't about the outcome. It was about the journey. And I was finally ready to take that journey on my own terms.

CHAPTER TWENTY-SEVEN

THE TURNING POINT

Time had passed, and the semester moved forward at its own pace. For the first time in 2 years of college, I didn't feel like I was living a life of obligations, commitments, or pressures. I didn't force myself to attend classes just because that's what everyone else was doing. I knew what I needed to do—what was important for me—and I was finally focused on my own purpose.

I had come to terms with the fact that I wasn't like most of my classmates. I wasn't racing toward internships or worrying about grades. I wasn't chasing what society or my family expected me to chase. I had embraced a different kind of life, one that revolved around building my startup and writing my memoir. And to maintain some balance, I had also started using weed more regularly.

The freedom I felt came with its own contradictions. I was becoming more productive in some ways, but I was also slipping into old habits. In the third year, the college gave us the option to have single rooms, and I jumped at the chance. Having a room to myself felt like a small victory—a space where I could think, work, and just be. The rooms were all located close to each other, and the room next to mine belonged to Peter.

Peter was someone who didn't care much about grades or academics. He was a free spirit, living life on his own terms. He was known for his "arts"—a master at crushing weed smoothly, mixing tobacco, and making perfect joints. His room was the go-to spot for anyone looking for weed, and it became my daily escape. Peter had this small box, a *kaju katli* box, where he kept all the essential equipment for weed preparation: rolling papers, a chillum, and a wooden crushing tool. There was also a tea strainer to finely sift the weed for the perfect texture.

In a way, Peter was the only person in the hostel who had his priorities straight. He didn't stress over grades or jobs. He didn't even care about anything other than enjoying life. For me, his room was a place to unwind, to take a break from the overwhelming pressure of building my startup. It became a routine: go to Peter's room, smoke, and then go back to my own room to work on Igloo or write my memoir.

As the days went by, my work on the startup and the memoir continued. The memoir writing slowed down a bit, but the work on Igloo never stopped. My focus had become crystal clear: I was determined to launch my site, the platform that I had poured so much of my energy into. I had originally set the goal of launching Igloo on my birthday, August 28th. But I wasn't ready. The website still had some kinks to work out, and I wanted it to be perfect. So, I pushed the launch date to September 28th. But once again, I found myself unable to meet the deadline.

After months of working on it, the pressure started to get to me. I had spent four months obsessing over Igloo. My focus was so intense that I even began to see lines of code in my dreams. But instead of feeling motivated by my progress, I became overwhelmed. My laptop had started to haunt me—it was as though I couldn't escape the work, no matter how much I tried.

Eventually, I realized that I needed a break. My mind was exhausted, and so was my body. I couldn't continue at this pace without burning out. At the same time, mid-term exams were approaching, and I knew I needed to focus on those as well. So, I made the decision to step away from Igloo for a while. I would take a break and focus on my exams.

The day of the mid-term exams arrived, and for the first time in my IIT life, I didn't feel any pressure. I didn't feel the need to study endlessly or cram the night before. I didn't care about the results. I had come to a realization that had completely shifted my perspective: **I had found my purpose in life.** And that purpose wasn't tied to exams, grades, or the traditional path everyone else was following.

I entered the exam hall without any stress. I knew I wouldn't perform well, and honestly, I didn't care. And true to my expectation, I performed poorly in most of my exams. But strangely, I didn't feel defeated. There was no anger, no disappointment. I was at peace with my decision. For the first time in years, I wasn't living for validation. I was living for myself, and that was enough.

The semester ended, and it was time for the final exams. I didn't change my approach—still not studying the way I used to, still not worrying about the results. I wrote my exams, packed my bags, and headed home, hoping for the best. When the results came out, I passed all of my exams except one, which required a re-examination. That, too, didn't bother me.

I had reached a point in my life where I realized that failures and setbacks didn't define me. They were just part of the process. The real measure of success wasn't in grades, internships, or societal approval—it was in the pursuit of your passion, your dreams, and your true self.

During these months, I had discovered something about myself that I hadn't known before: I wasn't afraid of failure. I wasn't afraid of being different. I wasn't afraid of the unknown. I was building something that I believed in, something that had the potential to change the world. And that was enough to fuel me for the long journey ahead.

As I reflected on this period of my life, I realized that IIT was merely a stepping stone in my journey. It was a place where I had learned the basics of academic knowledge, but it was outside of those walls that I was truly learning what life was all about. The lessons I had gained were not from textbooks—they were from the experiences, the friendships, and the failures that shaped me into who I was becoming.

The journey wasn't over yet. There were still challenges ahead. There would still be times when I doubted myself or felt overwhelmed. But for the first time, I had found the courage to walk my own path, no matter how different it might seem from everyone else's. And I was finally at peace with that.

The future was uncertain, but one thing was clear: I had found my purpose. And that was all that mattered.